SUNSHIP III™

PERCEPTION AND CHOICE FOR THE JOURNEY AHEAD

BY
STEVE VAN MATRE
AND BRUCE JOHNSON

DESIGNED AND PRODUCED BY
THE INSTITUTE FOR EARTH EDUCATION

Cover by Margy O'Brien
Additional art by Margy O'Brien,
Jan Muir, and Matt Haag

Typesetting and Layout by
Erika Eschholz

First Printing, 1997

ISBN: 0-917011-03-1

Library of Congress: 96-80419

Published By
The Institute for Earth Education
Cedar Cove
Greenville, WV 24945
U.S.A.

DEDICATION

to the

McKeever Environmental Learning Center
who initiated the programme
and
Kris Mosher
who funded the publication

TABLE OF CONTENTS

Acknowledgements

The SUNSHIP III programme has been under development for almost fifteen years. While all of our model earth education programmes undergo several years of development and piloting before they are published, this one has taken especially long due to the fact that we have not been able to work on it with the kind of focused, sustained effort that we would have liked. Lack of funding, the pressing needs of developing the organization and limited pilot sites for a couple of years have meant that our efforts, while substantial, have been a bit sporadic.

Thanks to the work of numerous people, those listed below and all of the others who worked as staff at the various pilot sites, we finally have a programme we feel is ready to implement. While we know it is not perfect, and as we do with all of our model programmes, we will continue polishing it, we know that this is a powerful experience for the early teens. More than any of our other model programmes, SUNSHIP III weaves the messages of conservative energy and materials use, plus their requisite lifestyle changes, throughout the entire experience.

Our thanks should begin at the start, with the efforts of Dick Touvell, Deb Lyons and Randall Weisenmayer at the McKeever Environmental Learning Center in Sandy Lake, Pennsylvania. They had been offering our Sunship Earth programme for some time and wanted something similar for young teens. They approached us about developing a programme to be offered in June, 1982.

In late 1981 and early 1982, Kirk Hoessle, working with Steve Van Matre, headed up an effort of our staff Associates in Washington and Oregon to develop seven Conceptual Encounters. These were

i

developed further by Steve's environmental interpretation and education students, and later by Mike Mayer and Steve who added a new series of Immersing Experiences and Discovery Parties. In June of that year, Jeff McFadden, Fran Bires and I headed to the McKeever Center and ran the programme with the help of Deb, Randy, Nancy Bires, Dave Falvo and others. Later that summer, Fran and Nancy Bires, Jeff McFadden and I ran the programme at the Ryerson Conservation Area in suburban Chicago with the help of Mike Mayer and Tudi Arneil. Those initial efforts convinced us that we had the makings of a good programme, but we realized we had a lot of work to do as well.

In the spring of 1983, after making further revisions, Steve's graduate students, Laurie Farber, Karen Gartland Murray, Dori Bovard and Dave Marshal, ran another pilot in Chicago with the help of Roger Tucker and the Heller Interpretive Center.

For the next couple of years, our only pilots were at the McKeever Center, which ran the programme for only one or two sessions each year. We continued with development sessions, however, out of which came a whole new "hooker" and "organizer", new activities and the decision to focus on the "Big Four" earth education concepts — energy flow, cycling, interrelationships and change.

The McKeever Center has continued to pilot the programme each year. They were joined in 1986 by the Rocky Mountain YMCA and the Calgary Board of Education in Alberta. Ron Sweet, Mike Walters, Gary Rasberry and Megan Jentz headed up that effort assisted by Matt Daw, Rob Hall, Gina Lemire and a host of others.

In 1989, two Australian sites began piloting the programme. Birrigai Outdoor School in the Australian Capitol Territory has run SUNSHIP III for several sessions each year since then. Doug Coreau, Arthur Baker, Peter Blunt, Shirley Campbell, Kerri Thompson and Steve Rudd put their many talents and great reserves of energy to work in its behalf. The Scott's Creek Field Centre of Prince Alfred College in South Australia also has run the programme each year since 1989. Bill and Kathy Coutts and Martyn and Sonya Risbey have been the driving force behind that effort.

In 1991, YMCA Camp Wanakita in Ontario and Karatta Outdoor School on Kangaroo Island in South Australia began additional pilots. Dave Newnham, Todd Fyfe, John Munro, and Diane Stewart in Ontario and Bill Prime on Kangaroo Island were the key people at those sites.

Frank Chapman Centre in Worcestershire, England has also been running the programme for the last few years. John Rhymer, Tony and Rosemary Winnall and John Milner have been coordinating that effort. Martin Paine also contributed some important insights.

Artists Margy O'Brien, Matt Haag and Jan Muir once again put their talents to work to create the illustrations and graphics used in the programme and in this book. Dave Wampler, in addition to helping in the early development of the Conceptual Encounters, designed and guided the accompanying set of **Conceptual Encounters** through their publication in 1991. Dave White drafted the overviews of the Conceptual Encounters found here. Erika Eschholz designed and produced this piece as well as the masters used by those running the programme. Laurie Farber provided much needed technical support, and Ed Paschich scanned the illustrations for us.

With so many involved over such a long time, it is difficult to keep track of who was responsible for which specific ideas or components. Solarville, The Cycle Factory and The Museum Project activities began with the original team in 1981. The Cycle Factory in particular hasn't changed much, though we now use cosum or whiffle balls rather than balloons!

Fran, Jeff and I developed the first version of the Endangered Species Ceremony at the McKeever Center in 1982, the Birrigai team created the Billy's Day skit, the Rocky Mountain YMCA folks came up with the idea of using cosum balls for The Cycle Factory, Gary Rasberry and Matt Daw took on the very successful but rather daunting task of being the first to play P/C... the list could go on and on for many pages.

Steve Van Matre has remained the main idea force throughout the history of the programme. His gift of creativity, ability to come up with "hookers" and "organizers" and sixth sense about what will work continues to amaze me. At our development sessions we like to send Steve to bed with a good problem to solve, knowing that he will invariably rise early and, often while in the shower, come up with the answer. (Sometimes it helps to have had a few cups of coffee to be ready for those answers; I'll never forget the time he came up with the P/C skit. I think we all wondered if he'd finally lost it, but it works beautifully and is much the same as he originally described it to us in great detail early one morning in the Jemez Mountains of New Mexico.)

Fran Bires has been another constant throughout the development of SUNSHIP III. While my main task over the years has been to flesh out and write-up the initial drafts of the activities and materials we have come up with in our development sessions, communicate with and visit pilot sites, and so on, Fran has been the one who has had to implement all of the wild ideas. His efforts on SUNSHIP III and other earth education programmes continue to be substantial, and his voice on the other end of the phone, providing good, practical advice, keeps me going.

Nancy Bires is a bundle of energy who has not only been involved with SUNSHIP III pilots as an activity leader but as a teacher bringing students to the programme and working with them on the follow-through.

Jeff McFadden, in addition to his excellent rapport with participants, has an uncanny ability to get to the core of an idea and see if it really does the job we want it to do. He is great at keeping us on track.

Peter Blunt, our Australian Programme Coordinator, has done an incredible job of communication. In an organization as dependent as ours is on volunteer efforts, waiting to hear from people who may have to write their comments about an activity in the wee hours of the morning, communication can be very frustrating. Peter has been amazingly thorough and timely in keeping us posted on the Australian piloting efforts and results as well as keeping me on my toes with his requests for information and revised write-ups.

Arthur Baker, at the Birrigai Outdoor School, not only lent his support and help over several years of piloting, his keen eye helped us get rid of some of the "Americanisms".

As he has so often done before, Donn Edwards reviewed the manuscript, providing valuable editorial comments.

Monica Held stepped forward to arrange sources for materials needed to run the programme, including everything from the fishhook and wristband each participant receives to the slides used in the Commencement.

In the end, though, it was a timely and generous loan from longtime Associate Kris Mosher that has enabled us to get this programme out to you.

A special thanks must also go to my family. My wife, Marg, and my children, Tanner and Laurel, have patiently put up with weekend development sessions and late nights on the computer for many years.

Of course, there have been countless others who have been involved in running the program at these pilot sites over the last fifteen years or have looked over materials and given us their comments. A few of them are mentioned here. Please forgive us if we have inadvertently forgotten someone's contribution.

Karen Bushor   Brendon Cartledge   Gael Hughes
Eddie Soloway   Jim Wells

Finally, we must thank all of our members around the world. Their support contributes to all of our programme development efforts.

It has been a joy to work with so many talented, hard-working leaders. I look forward to getting many more involved in the future as more SUNSHIP III programmes get underway.

Bruce Johnson
Corrales, New Mexico

INTRODUCTION

Welcome to the pages of our fourth major programme for helping young people live more lightly on the earth. **SUNSHIP Earth**™, **Earthkeepers**™ and **Earth Rangers**™ for the 10-11 year olds were the first three, but this one's for the 13-14 year olds. We think it's our best effort so far, an adventuresome, yet intellectually challenging romp through the reasons and rewards for crafting a more ecological lifestyle.

SUNSHIP III is about perception and choice in our daily habits and routines. It is about exploration and discovery in the larger context of where and how we live. And it is about examining alternatives and making sacrifices on behalf of a healthier home planet.

We called it SUNSHIP III because we inhabit the third planet orbiting that nondescript, medium-sized star we call the sun. For us, it is our **S**hip **O**f **L**ife.

Right from the beginning, we signal our participants in this programme that their early teens will represent one of the most important periods on board this vessel for them, because of the decisions they will be making during these years about their energy and materials use, and how they will relate with the other life that shares this "sunship" with them. We suggest there's a fork in the path ahead (represented in the programme's logo), and they must decide soon whether to follow a consumptive or conservative route in crafting their own lifestyle on board.

In The Institute for Earth Education we are determined to design carefully-crafted springboard experiences that will captivate and motivate learners, then catapult them back to their homes and schools where the real changes must take place if we are to address the environmental problems we face. Surprisingly, when it came to 13-14 year olds, this turned out to be a much tougher task than we anticipated. SUNSHIP III has been designed, then redesigned, several times over the past decade. It took several of those years just to figure out how to "hook" or motivate a fourteen year old! The early teens represent a time of life so crowded with demands and desires and dreams, all jostling for immediate attention, that it's often next to impossible to be heard above the din.

Since we have always maintained in earth education that we want to pull our learners, not push them, the question for us became, how could we pull young teens into participating enthusiastically in learning to live more lightly on the earth? After struggling with this problem for several years, the solution turned out to be fairly simple. We decided not to treat them like teenagers at all; we elected to treat them as adults.

Furthermore, we set out to congratulate them on arriving at their new elevated status. So SUNSHIP III begins with an introduction to the rites of passage incorporated traditionally in the fabric of indigenous cultures, but now missing in many of our contemporary societies. (Of course, we don't presume to be serving that function, but we do want to set the stage for why we are asking our participants to rise up and take more responsibility for their own actions.) Shortly after hearing about some of these coming of age experiences, our participants receive a congratulatory card and an invitation to attend a most unusual "Commencement" exercise.

Perhaps I should back up for a moment and explain that in earth education we design our programmes based upon three broad phases of human development that we refer to as the three I's: imitative, imaginative, intellectual. In the beginning, young children want most of all to be able to duplicate the actions of the adults around them. They love to play with adult things, particularly when scaled down for them, and will spend hours talking such items into some sort of pattern or story. However, at about the same time they lose their baby teeth, imitation gives way to imagination. Now it's those larger than life heroes that capture their attention, and gradually, fantasy takes on an ever greater role for them. Generally, all this gets more grounded again at about the same time as puberty, when the intellectual phase of development takes over. The life of the mind becomes more important then as young teens spend untold hours talking about the new social circles and interactions they share.

Consequently, for the new teenager, the best motivator is often something that appeals to both the imaginative and intellectual phases, particularly when the emphasis is on physically moving beyond the home setting. Young teens are beginning to wean themselves away from their families during this time, but in doing so run the risk of bonding excessively with a group of their peers instead. Powerful forces in music, fashion, sports, etc. can end up dominating their lives to the exclusion of all else. In SUNSHIP III we would like to support this natural desire to reach out to a larger community, but to suggest alternative ways for doing so. We want to encourage independence within an interdependent context rather than a newly dependent one.

Unfortunately, any attempt to provide a more sophisticated sense of adventure, couched as it were in a stronger intellectual framework, runs the risk of being seen on occasion as a threat by those who strive for purity in a particular religious perspective. We regret this. For the most part, we don't want our metaphors and analogies to be taken literally, but merely to suggest for the learners a certain richness of experience that awaits them.

When we refer to the "Temple of SOL" in an activity focusing on the concept of interrelationships, for example, it is not because we want to introduce our participants to some arcane religious group, but because we want to get their attention and hold it long enough to make our point.

As an organization the institute takes no particular religious stance, and we surely don't want to offend those who do. The Institute for Earth Education has always taken the position that people should look within their own religious perspectives for the seeds of a more ecologically harmonious relationship with the earth, that they should nurture those found there, then share them with others. We are convinced that all the world's great religions contain such seeds, and many are already sprouting and taking hold in our societies.

Nonetheless, when you couple some of the evocative adjectives often in use today in nature education, such as, magical, enchanting, mysterious, etc. with our attempts to create captivating images for our activities, such as the Temple of SOL in this programme, it often makes it sound even worse, arousing suspicion among some of those who don't understand our motives (and even among a few who do!). We hope we can gain your support in clarifying what we are trying to accomplish and why we are going about it as we are.

Young teens are captivated by stories that involve making personal choices, particularly when those stories take place in what they perceive to be exotic settings. Actually, teens are immersed now in such examples in both their educational and recreational activities most every day. However, if you feel there are elements of our programme that may offend some parents, you would probably be better off to discuss this with them beforehand rather than going ahead and hoping they won't notice.

In addition, there are some folks who object to our term, "Magic Spot", for characterizing a quiet time alone in a natural setting. When we began using this term over 20 years ago, it was because we wanted to convey that the natural world is a wondrous place, brimming with discoveries, for those who merely take the time to sit quietly and tune into the flow of life around them. We certainly had no supernatural motive in mind, but simply wanted to help people experience the joy of being outside immersed in a natural community. Today, the word magic has become synonymous in popular usage with anything a bit out of the ordinary or possessing that wondrous, sparkling quality we call awe, so it still fits well within our original objectives. Undoubtedly, the easiest thing to do when people object to this term would be simply to change it to "Quiet Spot" instead, but in many cases we think you could accomplish more by letting people know in the beginning what you are doing and why. Surely, the word magic does not have to be confined in our vocabulary to those things which are seen as supernatural or evil (or eliminated entirely because someone fears such a connection).

Sometimes in our work we also use symbols or terms that have other meanings in other contexts. We don't do this deliberately; we are merely trying to create exciting learning adventures for our participants, or easily remembered labels for our leaders, and inadvertently come up with such ideas in the process. However, not surprisingly, once we have come up with something that works, we are reluctant to go back and dump it just because someone else uses the same symbol or term in a different way. Please don't forget that most of the images and imagined characters in our programmes are put forth with a twinkle in the eye. The learners sense that they are being "set up", but they are more than ready to go along with this when they discover it means stimulating learning experiences lie ahead. In SUNSHIP III the learners understand right away that this is a participatory adventure yarn; it's the MTV of outdoor learning. As one of our leaders expressed it, parts of the programme are a video game come to life. It's not something to be taken literally, but figuratively.

For example, we use the analogy of a fish in SUNSHIP III because lots of young people at this age spend a fair amount of time daydreaming. So we chose the image of a fish to represent the kinds of choices they are called upon to make in those dreams. Then we ask them to pull this image out now and then and examine it. On one side the scales of the fish contain short statements about the things they will not do environmentally and on the other the things they will. In short, what kinds of environmental behaviours they will pursue or avoid in their daily lives. In this case, we wanted them to think about how they will relate with the other life of the earth, but it's clear that they will also consider other choices they are making in their lives as well. Naturally, we hope that this would serve to help, not hinder, what their families wish for them.

Teens have moved beyond stories that begin, "Once Upon a Time...", only in their sociological development, not their inner desire. As adults we are all captivated by tales of those who live in a quite different world, yet face the same problems we do. Someone has referred to our contemporary, imaginative realm of adult books and films and plays as "ever-ever land". It's a place we can go to gain fresh perspectives, timeless insights or the courage to continue our own struggles.

Whether we like to admit it or not, young teens are out there testing their own environmental truths most every day. We believe that it will be helpful to them to see that they are not alone in this. It is a natural part of growing up. If it seems like SUNSHIP III has set sail for "ever-ever land" at times, it's in the hope that we can hold the attention of these learners long enough to consider some very important questions about their impact upon the earth.

Naturally, we hope we will be able to continue developing highly engaging learning experiences like these without creating unnecessary problems for the leaders and parents of our learners. We don't want to get in anyone's way, but we are convinced that learning to "live more lightly" on the earth remains one of the most urgent educational needs of our time, and thus demands the most powerful learning experiences we can muster.

Okay. This has been a lengthy justification, and I hope I haven't scared anyone off about what's coming. We think you will enjoy this programme as much as we have in designing it.

Finally, it has become more and more obvious over the years that all of our programmes are ongoing productions, and SUNSHIP III is no exception. We will continue improving it in the future and invite you to join us in doing so.

S.V.M.
Kentmere Valley, Lake District
United Kingdom

THE INSTITUTE FOR EARTH EDUCATION

⊕ LEARNING TO LIVE LIGHTLY ⊕

The Institute for Earth Education is a nonprofit volunteer organization made up of an international network of individual and member organizations. We believe that a special kind of education - EARTH EDUCATION - can make a significant difference in the health of our planet. Earth education is the process of helping people build an understanding of, appreciation for, and harmony with the earth and its life. All our activities and programmes are designed to help achieve this goal.

Founded in 1974, our work builds on the pioneering efforts documented in the **Acclimatization** and **Acclimatizing** books. However, since their publication in the early seventies, we have learned that a few environmental activities are not enough. There remains an urgent need for complete educational programmes - programmes that focus primarily on understanding basic ecological systems (such as energy flow, cycling and interrelationships), what these systems mean for people in their own lives and what they can do to begin living more in harmony with these systems which support all life on the planet earth. Today, The Institute for Earth Education has branches underway in Australia, Canada, Finland, France, Germany, Italy, Japan, the United Kingdom and the United States.

The major work of the institute is to design and disseminate specific educational programmes that change people's view of our home, the planet earth, and the way they interact with its natural systems and communities. **Sunship Earth**, our first complete programme (designed for upper elementary students), has achieved widespread attention since it first appeared in 1980. Outdoor leaders around the world have called it the most focused, innovative and hard-hitting educational programme of its kind ever produced. In 1987 we followed it up with a shorter experience for the same age, *Earthkeepers*. And today, we are working on a number of programmes for both younger and older participants.

WHYS, WHATS & WAYS OF EARTH EDUCATION

Earth education is the process of helping people live more harmoniously and joyously with the natural world. And we have divided the overall structure of that process into three parts: the Whys, the Whats and the Ways. Each of the three combine to form the supporting pyramid for the process of helping others build an understanding of, appreciation for and harmony with the earth and its life.

Why earth education? Simply because the human passengers on board the planet earth are endangering most other living things that share the planet with them and their own life support systems in the process. As a result, earth advocates are desperately needed to serve as teachers and models and to champion the existence of our fellow non-human passengers. We also believe that people who have broader understandings and deeper feelings for the planet as a vessel of life are wiser and healthier and happier themselves.

What does it include? Understandings, feelings and processings are the key components of the earth education edifice. In order to live more in harmony with other life on our planet, people first need a basic understanding of its ecological systems and communities. Next, they must feel a deep and abiding emotional attachment to all life. And finally, they must begin processing their new understandings and feelings by making changes in their own lifestyles.

How is it accomplished? First, careful structuring provides the framework for adventuresome, magical learning activities that focus on these specific outcomes. Second, earth education immerses its participants in lots of rich, firsthand contact with the natural world. And third, its participants are encouraged to relate these experiences to their own lives by providing them with time to be alone in natural settings where they can reflect upon both the other life around them and their own environmental habits. Most important, an earth education programme has to be completed in specific actions in the home and school setting.

THE WHYS

•• ━━━ **Preserving**
We believe the earth as we know it is endangered by its human passengers.

•• ━━━ •• ━━━ **Nurturing**
We believe people who have broader understandings and deeper feelings for the planet as a vessel of life are wiser and healthier and happier.

•• ━━━ •• ━━━ •• ━━━ **Training**
We believe earth advocates are needed to serve as environmental teachers and models, and to champion the existence of earth's nonhuman passengers.

THE WHATS

•• ▬▬ **Understanding**
We believe in developing in people a basic comprehension of the major ecological systems and communities of the planet.

•• ▬▬ •• ▬▬ **Feeling**
We believe in instilling in people deep and abiding emotional attachments to the earth and its life.

•• ▬▬ •• ▬▬ •• ▬▬ **Processing**
We believe in helping people change the way they live on the earth.

THE WAYS

•• ▬▬ **Structuring**
We believe in building complete programmes with adventuresome, magical learning experiences that focus on specific outcomes.

•• ▬▬ •• ▬▬ **Immersing**
We believe in including lots of rich, firsthand contact with the natural world.

•• ▬▬ •• ▬▬ •• ▬▬ **Relating**
We believe in providing individuals with time to be alone in natural settings where they can reflect upon all life.

⊕ EARTH EDUCATION ⊕ PROGRAMMES

An Earth Education Programme is a skillfully crafted, sequential learning experience designed to help participants live more harmoniously and joyously with the earth and all its life.

We believe a learning programme, as opposed to a collection of randomly strung together, dissimilar activities, is more focused on and committed to its outcomes. A good programme provides the intrinsic motivation necessary to pull the learners into a sequence of cumulative activities designed to achieve an overall objective. It involves the learners in interactive and dynamic ways. And in the end, it is synergistic - all the pieces interact together in such a way that the whole becomes more than the sum of its parts.

Gathering up a bunch of unrelated activities available in our field and calling them a programme is like recording a batch of unrelated sounds and calling them a symphony. We strive to make an earth education programme a carefully crafted symphony on living more harmoniously and joyously with the earth.

PRESERVING

WHYS

NURTURING

TRAINING

Characteristics of an Earth Education Programme

An earth education programme:

⊕ Hooks and pulls the learners in with magical experiences that promise discovery and adventure.

⊕ Proceeds in an organized way to a definite outcome that the learners can identify beforehand and rewards them when they reach it.

⊕ Focuses on building good feelings for the earth and its life through lots of rich, firsthand contact.

⊕ Emphasizes major ecological understandings (at least four must be included: energy flow, cycling, interrelationships, change).

⊕ Gets the description of natural processes and places into the concrete through tasks that are both "hands-on" and "minds-on".

⊕ Uses good techniques in building focused, sequential, cumulative experiences that start where the learners are mentally and ends with lots of reinforcement for their new understandings.

⊕ Avoids the labeling and quizzing approach in favor of the full participation that comes with more sharing and doing.

⊕ Provides immediate application of its messages in the natural world and later in the human community. Pays attention to the details in every aspect of the learning situation.

⊕ Transfers the learning by completing the action back at school and home in specific lifestyle tasks designed for personal behavioural change.

SUNSHIP III OVERVIEW

⊕ SCHEDULE ⊕

Pretrip
4 weeks ahead (sent to school)
- a large envelope for each student containing a letter of explanation and a Life Inventory (to be completed and sent to the centre)

3 weeks ahead (sent to school)
- congratulations cards
- invitations to commencement
- gift cheques

2 weeks ahead (classroom visit)
- Guidebooks
- chequebooks
- Readiness Checks (to be completed and brought to the centre)

Day 1

10:30 am	Arrival
10:45	Commencement - opening (Ledgers distributed)
11:30	Registration/Site Tour/ Lunch - rotation
1:30 pm	"Solarville"
3:00	Magic Spots
3:30	Sharing Circles
4:00	Time Out
6:00	Dinner (pizza)
7:00	Daily Lifestyle Analysis, Sharing Circles
8:00	Campfire

Day 2

8:00 am	Breakfast
9:00	"Cycle Factory"/"Museum Project"/ "Objet Trouvé" (part one) - rotation (1½ hrs. each)

noon	Lunch
1:00pm	Sharing Circles
1:30	(continue morning rotation)
3:00	"Objet Trouvé" (part two)/Magic Spots/ Time Out - rotation (½ hour each)
4:30	"Objet Trouve" (part three)
5:30	Dinner
6:00	Time Out
7:00	Daily Lifestyle Analysis, Sharing Circles
8:00	"Temple of SOL" (part one)

Day 3

predawn	Endangered Species Ceremony
8:00 am	Breakfast
9:00	"Temple of SOL" (part two)
10:30	Magic Spots
11:00	Commencement - closing (maps and wristbands distributed)
11:30	Sharing Circles

Follow-through

Quest

Sharing Circles (held at school)

Presentation of medallions at the Temple of SOL

NOTES, CUES AND PROPS

•• This schedule is set up for 3 groups of 15-20 students per group. If you have fewer (or more) groups, the schedule can be easily adjusted. However, the programme components should be done in the same order.

•• On the first day, there is a rotation among lunch, registration and the site tour. This is because registration gets bogged down easily if there are too many participants waiting in line.

•• The Endangered Species Ceremony is designed to be held at dawn. An alternative time for the activity would be on the evening of the first day at dusk.

Hookers and Organizers

In earth education the "hooker" is the initial experience that sets the students up to want to participate in the learning activity. We always said in our Acclimatization work that we wanted to pull the learners, not push them. So the hooker is the motivator. It's what pulls the learners in and motivates them to want to carry out the learning tasks we have established. A hooker turns a boring worksheet into an exciting task. A hooker turns an authoritarian leader into a learning helper. A hooker turns the listless student into an energetic participant. A hooker can be as elementary as a special invitation and map delivered to a classroom before an adventure, or it can be as elaborate as our "Welcome Aboard" ceremony in Sunship Earth.

The "organizer" is a device that helps the participants hold onto the points learned. It can be as simple as using the word HOMES to remember the names of the Great Lakes of North America: Huron, Ontario, Michigan, Erie, Superior. Or, it can be as complicated as EC-DC-IC-A, the formula we use in Sunship Earth for explaining the ecological story of life on our planet (E = Energy Flow, C = Cycles, D = Diversity, C = Community, I = Interrelationships, C = Change, A = Adaptation).

The overall hooker of the SUNSHIP III programme is the invitation to attend the annual Commencement Exercises; exercises that will include an intense, captivating presentation on perception and choice. This opening provides the context within which everything else takes place.

The organizer that helps the learners keep track of what they are learning in the programme is the term SOL, which represents the **S**ystems, **S**ections and **S**tyles **O**f **L**ife on board the sunship we share.

TRAINING - PHASE I

⊕ PRETRIP PREPARATIONS ⊕

A few weeks before participating in the SUNSHIP III programme, the class receives a packet from the sponsoring centre. It contains large envelopes, one for each student. Among the items inside the students find the following letter:

Dear _____,

I am writing because you are approaching a major change in your life. Right now is a crucial time because up until this point others have been making the most important decisions for you. Soon you will be making more and more decisions for yourself. Your childhood is about to end and adolescence begin.

You may have already heard of a Commencement Exercise. To commence means to begin. When you graduate from school, the ceremony to mark that transition from school to the next stage in life is called a Commencement. Our society has ceremonies to mark many changes in life — graduation, marriage, promotion and so on, but seems to have forgotten that important step from childhood to adolescence. We think this change is so important that we have prepared a special Commencement Exercise for it, but before we invite you to attend, we need to find out if you are ready for this stage in your life.

Enclosed you will find a "Life Inventory". Please take some time to fill it out carefully. Your teacher will send it back to us to look over.

Sincerely,

Peter Blunt

In the envelopes the students find the Life Inventory asking them to think about what they have learned and experienced so far in their lives.

LIFE INVENTORY

for _____

This inventory is meant to be a check to see if you are ready to commence the next stage of your life. There are no right or wrong answers. Please respond to each question as completely as possible.

Skills

People acquire many skills in childhood. Please tick (check) those that apply to you. Having a skill does not mean that you are an expert at it or even very good at it; it simply indicates that you can do it. Some of these skills you've had for a long time; others may be more recent. Some may seem incredibly easy now, but that is only because you are older and have learned much more; at the time they were learned they may have seemed very hard. (You do not need to have all of these skills to be ready for the next stage of life, but you will probably have many of them.)

____ talking *	____ listening
____ reading	____ writing
____ walking	____ running
____ swimming	____ riding a bike
____ following directions	____ giving directions
____ reading a map	____ telling time

____ adding & subtracting   ____ multiplying & dividing

____ handling money   ____ tying your shoelaces

____ playing games   ____ playing sports

____ fixing your own lunch   ____ making a phone call

____ cleaning your room   ____ planting seeds

____ taking care of a pet   ____ washing the dishes

____ singing   ____ telling a story

____ telling jokes   ____ drawing a picture

____   ____

____   ____

____   ____

* It seems strange to start here, but did you know that this is
probably the most difficult thing anyone ever learns to do?

Influences

Who have been the most important people in your life
— parents, brothers/sisters, grandparents, teachers, friends?
Write down a few people who have made a big difference in your
life and describe how they have done so. You should try to list at
least two, but you can list more if you like.

Person:_____

Why?_____

_____

Person:_____

Why?_____

_____

Person:_____

Why?_____

_____

Person:_____

Why?_____

_____

Interests

What are the things that interest you the most right now?

_____

_____

What things interested you the most when you were 9 or 10 years old?

_____

_____

What things interested you the most when you were 5 or 6 years old?

_____

_____

Decisions   ━━━ •• ━━━

What things right now do you decide for yourself?

_____

_____

What things do others decide for you?_____

_____

_____

Do you make more decisions than you did when you were 5 or 6 years old? _____ If so, what kinds of things do you decide now that you couldn't then?

_____

_____

What things do you wish you could decide for yourself?

_____

_____

Impact

Do you recycle anything? _____

If so, what? _____

Do you throw away much food at meals? _____

Do you leave the water on more than you need to when brushing your teeth or washing your hands? _____

Do you leave lights on in rooms when you leave them? _____

Do you spend most of your free time inside or outside? _____

Do you explore natural places very often? _____

Do you have a garden? _____

Do you ever ask not to be given a bag when buying something at a store? _____

Do you use lots of electronic games? _____

Thank you for taking the time to fill out this inventory. Your teacher will send it to us to evaluate to see if you are indeed ready for the next stage of your life. If you are, you will be hearing from us soon.

Each student completes the Life Inventory, and the teacher send the forms off to the centre. A week later, each student receives a congratulations card (congratulating him or her on being ready for the next stage in life), a gift cheque for 1,000 Solarians (to be used to pay for the exercises) and an invitation to the Commencement. They are all put into the large envelope that contained the initial letter.

The teacher divides the class into "Sharing Circle" groups. These are teams of ten to fifteen students who will be working together in several different aspects of the programme. The teacher is careful to choose a good mix of students who will be able to function well as a group.

The Guidebook contains descriptions of SUNSHIP III, a Ship Of Life. Beginning with a blueprint showing the Systems Of Life and some of our planet's Sections Of Life, the Guidebook also includes information on care and maintenance, a warranty, technical terms with definitions, a description and illustration of each of the four Systems Of Life, as well as of the Sections Of Life, Styles Of Life and Stages Of Life. In addition to providing background information before the Commencement Exercises, the Guidebook is used during the exercises as well.

Soon after that, a staff member from the centre visits the class. In addition to explaining what the centre is like, what items to bring, and answering questions, she has a Guidebook, a Readiness Check and a chequebook for each student. Essentially, the Guidebook is a learning tool that explains the Systems Of Life on the sunship, the basic ecological processes that form the conceptual understandings of the programme. The participants read the Guidebooks at school and then take the Readiness Check.

The Readiness Check contains questions about the basic understandings contained in the Guidebook. Each student completes the check, but his or her score is averaged with those of other people in the Sharing Circle group. The group must get an average of at least 80% correct in order to attend the Commencement. Those groups who do not get that many correct on the first try work together to prepare for another attempt. For each percentage point above 80% everyone in the group will receive five extra Solarians at the Commencement Registration. (While most groups get well above that average the first time, it provides an opportunity for the participants to help each other acquire the basic information they need.)

Soon the class is ready for the Commencement Exercises. Armed with their personal envelopes containing the congratulations card, gift cheque, invitation, chequebook and Readiness Check, the participants board the bus.

NOTES, CUES AND PROPS

•• If a classroom visit is not possible, the Guidebooks, Readiness Checks and chequebooks can be mailed to the class.

•• The purpose of the life inventory is not to accept or reject participants but to get the participants to take stock of where they are in their lives.

TRAINING - PHASE II

⊕ COMMENCEMENT ⊕
(OPENING CEREMONY)

Upon arriving at the centre, the students are immediately led into a large meeting hall and seated in chairs facing a low stage or platform, with a lectern placed to one side. At the back a photograph of the earth as seen from space is projected onto a black wall in the centre of the stage. On either side of this there are black curtains. Shirley, one of the centre's staff, wearing a clay medallion impressed with the symbol of SOL, steps up to the spotlit lectern and greets them:

"Greetings... and congratulations. We are pleased to be able to welcome you on such an important occasion. Today you are "commencing", or beginning, one of the most important stages of your life as you pass from childhood to adolescence. Unfortunately, in many of our contemporary societies, people have forgotten to recognize and celebrate this important time in the lives of their young adults. So we have invited you to these special Commencement Exercises in honour of this important occasion in your own passage through one of the most challenging periods of human life.

"I have some letters here from people who couldn't attend today but still wanted to send their congratulations." (Shirley reads a couple of brief letters from people like the school superintendent, mayor or other important officials. One letter mentions a gift of a tree or shrub to be planted at the centre in honour of the occasion. At this point, another staff member comes up and presents a potted specimen to Shirley, which she places carefully next to the lectern.)

"The Commencement Exercises that begin this morning," Shirley explains, "will continue for the next 48 hours. You will explore and learn about our **S**hip **Of L**ife, this small, self-contained vessel on which we journey through space — the third planet from that medium-sized star we call the sun — our home, SUNSHIP III. Why? Because until now others have been making most of life's important decisions for you, but from this point on you will be making more and more of those decisions for yourself. And one of the most important decisions you ever make will be to sort out what kind of relationship you are going to have with the other life of the earth.

"You see, up until now you have been living in a certain way, in a sense following a predetermined path through life. You have been seeing, or perceiving, things along that path in a certain way as well. But there is a fork in the path ahead. We invited you to come here because we want to be sure you see and understand the choice. Many people don't see the second path; the way they perceive things only allows them to see the first one, the path most travelled. It is an easier path; it is broad and clear and seems relatively free of obstacles. The other path is worn and overgrown and mostly forgotten. It is more difficult to follow, but its rewards may be much greater.

"I am sure you have been hearing quite a bit about the environmental problems we seem to be facing more and more each year. We think that the reason we are swamped with them is because the way we live our lives is not in harmony with the way our planet works; our lifestyles don't fit our home. Most people don't understand how the ecological **S**ystems **O**f **L**ife operate here, how important the **S**ections **O**f **L**ife or natural communities are to the health of the planet, or how vital it is that we live a **S**tyle **O**f **L**ife that is in harmony with rather than disruptive of the natural world. The path most people follow provides a false sense of security, an illusion that we don't need to pay much attention to our impact on the sunship and that all will be well as long as a small number of people make lots of money.

"Frankly, we are going to try to change your perceptions during the next couple of days, to help you see through the illusions of our times and see that there is another path open to you. Much of what you will be doing will reveal the many ways we are dependent on and a part of the natural world. We hope to convince you to consider choosing the less travelled path, the one that is more in harmony with the natural systems and communities we share.

"So everything you do in the next 48 hours — from taking a shower in the morning to brushing your teeth at night — will be focused on two things: perception and choice; seeing things in a new way and making alternative choices for a new lifestyle. We will begin with your perception of our home, the planet earth."

Both the spotlight and the picture of the earth fade as the film "Powers of Ten" appears on the black wall (accompanied by some stirring background music). In a series of still frames, camera shots of the earth — pulling ever farther away from a picnic on the lawn to the farthest reaches of space — convey how we really exist on a small vessel in the immensity of the universe. At the end of the film, a spotlight comes up on Shirley at the podium, while the slide of the earth from space appears once again on the wall.

"Our planet is like a spaceship powered by the energy of the sun, so we call it a sunship. Since it is the third planet from the sun, we call it SUNSHIP III. It is our home, our only possible home. We hope to help you see it as an incredible, beautiful, wondrous home that needs our care.

"Part of what you will be doing here is finding out about the Systems Of Life that govern our sunship. You will visit Mario's Pizza Parlour in Solarville to learn about the power system, the flow of energy on board." (A circular slide of the pizza parlour replaces the earth image, followed by other circular slides showing a bit of what Shirley is talking about as she previews the three days they will spend at the centre. Of course, none of the slides gives away any of the surprises, but they help build curiosity about what's coming.)

"You will go to work at the Cycle Factory to discover the recycling system on board, sort through an old museum exhibit to learn about the time system here and visit the ruins of the Temple of SOL to see how everything is interrelated, the integrated circuits that govern our sunship.

"You will also get to explore some of the beautiful, natural Sections Of Life on board; the ecological communities of our sunship. Enroute, you will set up an art exhibit to illustrate your feelings about them and find your own Magic Spots where you can immerse yourself in the flow of life here.

"There are many things throughout this experience that you may not understand or even notice at first; these will become clearer as your perception changes. In fact, the SOL symbol itself" (illustrated on the screen first by a circular slide showing only the forked path, followed by another of the complete symbol) "has lots of rich meaning in it that you may already have discovered if you have paid close attention to my words so far.

"Those of us who wear the symbol of SOL, like this medallion around my neck, will be your Guides throughout these Commencement Exercises. We will be helping you see the choices that are available to you every day. In fact, you will begin making some of those decisions in a few minutes when you register, for you will be paying for all of the energy and materials you use here with the solarians you received as your commencement gift. You will have an opportunity to choose between using lots of energy and materials, and spending lots of solarians, or using less and saving solarians. The choices are up to you, but we will reward you for using less energy and materials and fine you for wasting them.

"Frankly, the next two days is actually a 'big set-up', including lots of surprises and special events. We have done this because we think it is important for you to learn how the earth works ecologically and to see how you can make choices that will have less impact on it. Here are some other people who feel the same."

The room returns to darkness and a series of circular slides of teenagers appears where the earth was on the black wall, accompanied by their taped comments (and natural background sounds) about this stage in their lives and the importance of trying to follow the other path. The spotlight comes up on Shirley again after the tape finishes. She merely says, "let's commence," and the room plunges into darkness once more.

For this part of the exercises a strange character, P/C, appears suddenly in front of the stage (representing a metaphorical amalgamation of the two sides of our own character, eco-harmonious and eco-disruptus). Two people of about the same height are securely tied back to back. They are wearing suit coats whose backs have been removed and are sewn together to make one costume. One coat is grey (disruptus) and the other green (harmonious). On their heads they wear black ski masks with a 12.5 cm (5 inch) round mirror sewn into the cloth just under the eyes, while the eye holes themselves have been covered with black

gauze. Black tights and tennis shoes complete the costume. By lifting their legs and letting the opposite person turn quickly around, first one side of the creature, then the other, can "spin" into view.

When P/C appears, the black curtain at the back of the stage on the opposite side of the lectern opens to reveal a chorus. The singers themselves cannot be seen, but the silhouetted shapes of a chorus in a chorus box are apparent. After a moment, it is obvious that most of the shapes are not real people but cut-outs.

"P/C"
(PERCEPTION AND CHOICE)

Scene 1 *(Chainsaw starts during blackout.)*

Disruptus appears (spotlight) shaking chainsaw and looking at it as if it's not working. The chainsaw dies.

Disruptus: **Well, dammit!** *(Tossing it into a rubbish bin.)* **That piece of junk's not working. Time to get another.**

(Blackout. Spin to reveal opposite character. Spotlight on.)

Harmonious: **Shhh! Shhh... Hear it?** *(Soft owl hoot is heard from a back corner of the room.)* **Gosh, I love that sound... here it comes...** *(louder owl hoot appears closer).*

(Blackout. Spin.)

(Disruptus appears in the spotlight with a pistol and fires a shot at the owl.)

(Blackout.)

(Spotlight comes up on a feather falling from overhead.)

(Blackout.)

*(Spotlight comes up on Harmonious bending down to put
its mirror right up to the face of a confederate seated in
the front row.)*

Harmonious: **Who do you see?**

Staff: **Uhhh... Me.**

Harmonious: **Who do you choose?**

(Blackout. Spin. Very quickly, this time.)

Staff: **Uhhh... yo...** *(starts to say you, then suddenly
realizes it's Disruptus again).*

(Blackout. Chorus sings "Perception and Choice" — first verse.)

Scene 2   *(P/C moves stage right)*

(Spotlight comes up on Harmonious who takes the lid off a jar and waves it around to release the smells.)

Harmonious: **Ooooouuhh!...** *(leaning down and holding the jar out to someone in the audience)* **smell this. I collected these smells this morning to remind me of the forest. I just took little pieces of things and put them together in my jar.**

(Blackout. Spin.)

Disruptus: *(Sticking a dead bird in front of the audience member's face)* **Look at this! I shot it this morning to add to my collection. I have birds now from all over this area.**

(Blackout. Spin.)

Harmonious: *(Bending down to a nearby confederate's face)* **Who do you see?**

Staff: **Me.**

Harmonious: **Who do you choose?**

(Blackout. Spin.)

Staff: **Uhhh...** *(freezes pointing at Disruptus)*

(Blackout. Chorus sings "Perception and Choice" — second verse.)

Scene 3   *(P/C moves stage left. Spotlight up on Harmonious.)*

Harmonious: *(Seeing walking stick leaning against lectern)* Wow!

What a nice walking stick. I've been looking for a new one. I

carry one when I'm out exploring. A walking stick can be a
really useful tool.

(Blackout. Spin.)

Disruptus: (Picking up
stick) **hey, look at this!**
(Slashing and jabbing the
stick like a sword, it lops
off the potted specimen
placed by the lectern
earlier by the
speaker.)

(Blackout.)

(P/C moves to edge
of audience and
Harmonious leans
down in the face of a
confederate.)

Harmonious: **Who do you see?**

Staff: **Me.**

Harmonious: **Who do you choose?**

(Blackout. Spin.)

Staff: **yo...**

(Blackout. Chorus sings "Perception and Choice" — third verse.)

Scene 4 (Spotlight up on Disruptus who pulls out a can of bug
spray.)

Disruptus: **They're some bugs in here. I've got just the
thing to kill those suckers!** (Bringing out several more kinds

of cans) **One of these will do the job...** *(Sprays)*

(Blackout. Spin.)

Harmonious: (Holding a large hand lens and looking at something in other hand) **Hey! Look at this! Whewww... I haven't seen one of these in a long time. What a beauty. You know, insects are some of the most amazing creatures on earth.**

(Blackout. Spin.)

(P/C moves to confederate and leans down face to face)

Disruptus: **Who do you see?**

Staff: **Me.**

(Blackout. Spin.)

Harmonious: **Who do you choose?**

(Blackout. Spin.)

Staff: (silence)

(Blackout. Chorus sings "Perception and Choice" — fourth verse.)

Scene 5

Disruptus: (Looking through shopping basket full of chemical supplies) **This is really great stuff. I just love these chemicals. Really eat the grime off things. Listen to this: sodium-o-benzyl-p-chloropenate and dimethyl benzyl ammonium chloride — great stuff, hey?**

(Blackout. Spin.)

Harmonious: (With picnic basket on red-checked cloth-covered table, laying out the items for the meal — no paper or plastic, or overly packaged foods, etc.) **I don't use any paper or plastics at my picnic. They represent a poor use of our energy and materials.** *(Slapping cheek)* **Drat those mosquitoes!**

Disruptus: (Passing spray can over shoulder) **Here, buddy. Try this...**

Harmonious: (Startled at the appearance of its other side) **No, uh, I don't think so...**

Disruptus: **Come on; it's great stuff — really works.**

Harmonious: **Uh, oh well, maybe just one spray.** *(Gives one spray, starts to hand it back, then puts it quickly into picnic basket.)*

(Blackout. Spin.)

Harmonious: **Who do you see?** *(Face to face with confederate.)*

Staff: **Me.**

Harmonious: **Who do you choose?** *(Blackout. Spin.)*

(Spotlight up on Disruptus. Freeze.)

(Blackout. Chorus sings "Perception and Choice" — fifth verse.)

Scene 6

Disruptus: (Looking at something closely) **Hey, what's this thing?**

Harmonious: (Passing hand lens over shoulder) **Here, use this.**

Disruptus: (Takes and uses hand lens) **Well, I'll be. This is okay. I would've never guessed you could see so much with one of these things. Will you look at that! Ha!** *(Starts to hand the lens back then surreptitiously slips it into a pocket.)*

(Blackout.)

Disruptus: (Face to face with confederate in audience) **Who do you see?**

Staff: **Me.**

(Blackout. Spin.)

Harmonious: **Who do you choose?**

(Blackout. P/C moves behind curtain. Chorus sings "Perception and Choice.")

The spotlight comes back up on Shirley at the podium (with the slide of the earth on the screen behind her). "Perception and Choice. Which side of that character will people of the future be like? Will we become Homo disruptus, mistreating our home and the other life that shares it with us? Or will we become Homo harmonious, living with the earth and its life in ways that sustain the planet? Both are really in all of us. But which side of us will be revealed in any situation? And which will become more dominant over our lifetime?

"The coming year will lay the foundation for the rest of your life. We hope the next 48 hours of this Commencement will reveal a new path for your life's journey, an alternative that you may not have known existed.

"To help you keep track of your thoughts throughout the Commencement, we have a gift for each of you — a special Ledger to use in recording what's happening to you during these exercises. As you leave the room, please step up here to receive it.

"Enjoy your journey, and save your Solarians."

SUNSHIP III.
LEDGER

The Ledger is a tool for participants to use in keeping track of their experiences both on site during the commencement and later while on the quest. It contains several sections including "My Choices" with places to record permit cost and keep track of the daily lifestyle analysis, "My Perceptions" for recording reflections on the experience of the commencement, "My Quest" for keeping track of personal experiences while on the quest and "My Lifestyle" for recording specific actions taken as a result of the commencement and the quest.

NOTES, CUES AND PROPS

•• Be sure to pause appropriately, and include nonverbal cues as well, to convey that all this is really a big "set-up". It's important that the learners understand they are being asked to engage mentally with what's happening.

•• Entry music — Paul Winter's "Sunsinger Theme" and "Hymn to the Sun". Exit music — Jim Scott's "Song for the Earth".

•• Sound and projection booth
     "Perception and Choice" tape (chorus)
     2 tape players with speakers
     Slides of programme activities
     Slide projector
     "Power of Ten" film
     Film projector
     Pin spotlight
     Taped comments by older teens & slides of them talking

- •• 1 lectern (podium)

- •• 1 black wall at centre stage for slides and film

- •• Letters from officials

- •• Tree or shrub

- •• Walking stick

- •• Ledgers

- •• Chorus Box (closed off from view until needed by a black curtain) to one side of stage — 3 to 4 cut out silhouettes and 1 or 2 staff members in the box — one of the tape players should be here with the "Perception and Choice" tape operated by one of the staff in the box.

- •• P/C suit, tights, ski masks with mirrors

- •• Chainsaw (working but with chain removed)

- •• Rubbish bin (containing a foam cushion to throw the chainsaw into)

- •• Feathers (and a system for letting them fall from the ceiling)

- •• Jar of smells

- •• Skin of a dead bird

- •• Insect sprays

- •• Imitation insect

- •• Large hand magnifying lens

- •• Picnic basket with checkered cloth & picnic items

•• Table on which to place the picnic basket, etc.

•• Plastic shopping bag with chemical cleaners

•• Small natural object

•• SOL medallions - for each staff member. These are worn instead of name tags at the opening and closing commencements only.

REGISTRATION

SUNSHIP III™

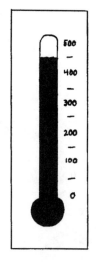

⊕ ORIENTATION ⊕
(TAKING STOCK)

REGISTRATION

After the opening of the Commencement Exercises, one of the three groups goes to lunch, another on a site tour and the third to registration. The latter group gathers in a room that has a SUNSHIP III poster and a disc with just the "Y" part of the SOL symbol hanging on the wall. There is also a large posterboard thermometer.

Bill steps to the front and greets the group. "We have a busy Commencement planned, so we need to get you registered as soon as possible. Let me explain a couple of things that may seem a bit strange. First, you need to pay for <u>all</u> of the energy and materials you use while you are here — all of them. That will not only begin changing your perceptions about energy and materials, it will require you to make some specific choices as well.

"The basic fee for the Commencement Exercises is 500 Solarians. That covers the energy and materials in your food, lodging and other needs that are already established for you. But there are other costs which you can control personally. Some of you may use quite a bit of energy and materials for those things while others use only a little. To be fair to everyone, rather than charging a flat fee for those costs, we are asking you to pay just for those you use. Saving Solarians is important, too. You will be able to use those you have left after the Commencement. We'll fill you in on that later.

"We use Solarians," Bill continues, "for all these costs because Solarians are units of sunlight energy. Since money is really just paper or metal representing a certain amount of energy, we use sunlight energy bills as our money here. "This chart," Bill explains as he points to the large thermometer, "shows 500 Solarians, the amount each of you will pay for the basic Commencement fee.

Throughout the next three days, you will notice the amount shown decrease as the Solarians (or energy), is used to keep us fed and housed and warm. It will be posted in the dining room where you can keep an eye on it."

Bill pulls out a permit card and holds it up for all to see. "This is a permit card. You must purchase permits each day to be able to use energy and materials for things like taking a shower, flushing a toilet or using a paper towel. All of those things involve energy and materials as well, so you need to pay for them. In a few minutes you will buy your first permit card. You will get to choose which things you want to do and that will determine how much your permit costs for today. However, be forewarned: if you do something you don't have a permit for, you can be fined double the cost of the permit for that item. So if you decide not to buy a permit for using paper towels to dry your hands, which would have cost you 10 Solarians for the day, and you go ahead and use one, you will be fined 20 Solarians instead. You will also be fined for wasting energy, like leaving the lights on in a room when you leave."

"Who is going to fine us?" asks a skeptical participant.

"Anyone," Bill answers. "Everyone will wear a permit card around his or her neck at all times, leaders too. The permit card will show what things you paid for on that day. Each of us will also wear a fine card." Bill holds one up. "It costs 100 Solarians and has 20 circles each worth 5 Solarians. Each Guide here — every teacher and leader — has a punch. If you get a 20 Solarian fine, a Guide will punch out 4 circles. At the end you can turn your fine card back in for a refund on the circles that aren't punched out."

"Can we fine the Guides?"

"Sure. And you can fine each other. But you won't have a punch. If you see someone that should be fined for something, anyone at all — even me — let a Guide know and they will 'punch them out'."

"Can we be fined for doing other things, like when my teacher yells at me for mucking around?"

"No, these fines aren't for that purpose; they are only for misusing or wasting energy or materials. And your teacher's role is a bit different this week too. Your teacher is here to guide you through these experiences marking a significant change in your life. You'll have to take care of the "mucking around" yourself.

Bill holds up a Ledger as he continues. "To help you keep track of all this, you have received a special Ledger. Be sure to keep it in your pouch along with your Guidebook and chequebook at all times."

Bill asks the group to take out their Ledgers and look through them. He also posts a list of the things they can get permits for and explains each item. Afterwards, the participants choose which permits they want to get for the first day, then write them down on the permit page for 'day one' in their Ledgers. Since the permits are for the whole day, they need to buy them for things they've already done that day as well as for those they will do the rest of the day. For example, if they took a shower before they came, they will need a permit for that, and so on.

As soon as the first participants are ready, they start through the registration line. There are four stations in the registration area, which is located outside the meeting hall they were just in. Each station has a table with the needed items and a sign telling what station it represents. Instructions are also posted at each table.

PERMITS
(MAKING CHOICES)

Station 1 — Registration

• Commencement Book — each participant signs in

• Shoulder pouch — to hold Guidebook, Ledger, chequebook, and pencil (each participant gets one) — collect large envelopes (to be returned at the end of the three days)

• Name tag - each participant must wear one at all times as identification for cashing cheques

• Sleeping rooms assigned (they move in right after finishing registration)

Station 2 — Permits

• Permit and fine cards distributed (on a cord to hang around the neck)

• Announce permits needed or desired (as recorded on Ledger page)

(A Guide stamps the ones chosen on the permit card, using a SOL symbol, and gives out an invoice showing the Solarians needed to pay for those permits.)

Station 3 — Cheques

- Write three cheques
  (commencement fee, fine card, permit invoice)

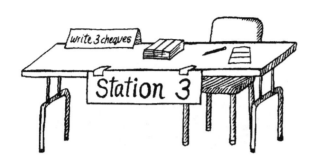

Station 4 — Cashiers

- Deposits and withdrawals — gift cheque is deposited by the cashiers and the other three cheques are entered as withdrawals

SITE TOUR
(CHANGING PERCEPTIONS)

To begin the tour, each group is taken to a large map that shows the site divided into "Sections Of Life" by thick black lines (marsh, meadow, forest, etc.) There are also some objects from special places, like a rock from a particular highlighted outcrop, displayed below the map. The participants are encouraged to find some of these places and explore these natural communities during their Time Out time.

LUNCH
(DEMONSTRATING BEHAVIOURS)

Mealtimes offer an excellent opportunity for demonstrating less consumptive ways of doing things. See our section on Support for suggestions and sources.

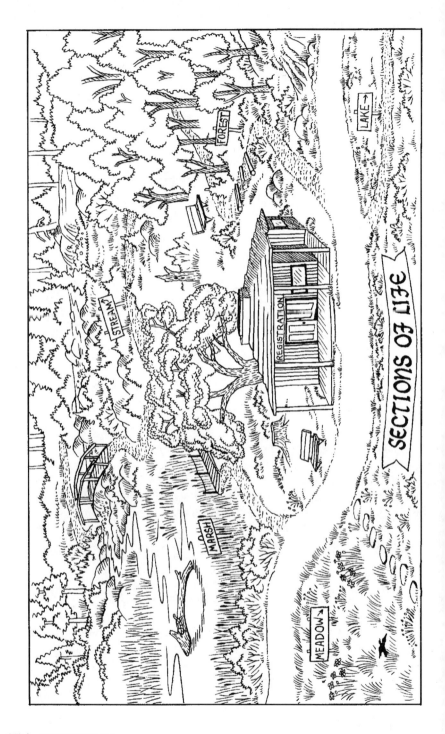

NOTES, CUES AND PROPS

Registration

Station 1 (Registration)
•• Instructions poster: 1) sign guestbook, 2) take a pouch, 3) take a name tag, 4) get a room, 5) go to permit station

Station 2 (Permits)
•• Instructions poster: 1) show Ledger permit page to registrar, 2) get an invoice for your permits, 3) put permit and fine cards around your neck, 4) take invoice to cheque writing station

Station 3 (Cheques)
•• (tables with pencils on chains and chairs to sit on) Large specimen examples of the three cheques that the participants must submit are on display on poster board for all to see and copy (one for 500 Solarians for the basic Commencement fee, one for 100 Solarians for the fine card and one for the total of their permit cost)

•• Instructions poster: 1) write a cheque for 500 Solarians for the basic Commencement fee, 2) write a cheque for 100 Solarians for the fine card, 3) write a cheque for the amount of Solarians shown on your permit invoice, 4) take all three cheques to the cashier along with your chequebook and your gift cheque of 1,000 Solarians

Station 4 (Cashiers)
•• Instructions poster: 1) give your gift cheque, the three cheques you wrote and your cheque book to a cashier, 2) when your chequebook is balanced, move into your assigned room

•• The number of leaders needed to supervise registration will vary depending on the number of people being registered, but be sure there are some people to help the participants move into their sleeping rooms as well.

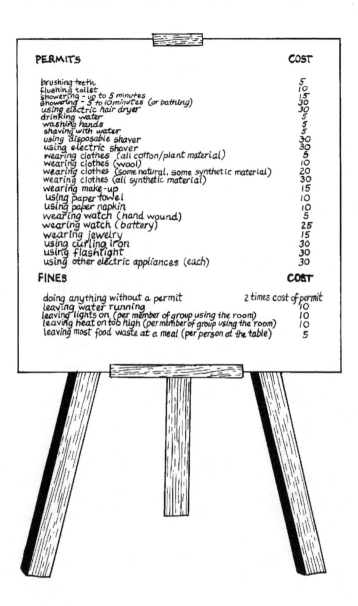

PERMITS	COST
brushing teeth	5
flushing toilet	10
showering - up to 5 minutes	15
showering - 5 to 10 minutes (or bathing)	30
using electric hair dryer	30
drinking water	5
washing hands	5
shaving with water	5
using disposable shaver	30
using electric shaver	30
wearing clothes (all cotton/plant material)	5
wearing clothes (wool)	10
wearing clothes (some natural, some synthetic material)	20
wearing clothes (all synthetic material)	30
wearing make-up	15
using paper towel	10
using paper napkin	10
wearing watch (hand wound)	5
wearing watch (battery)	25
wearing jewelry	15
using curling iron	30
using flashlight	30
using other electric appliances (each)	30

FINES	COST
doing anything without a permit	2 times cost of permit
leaving water running	10
leaving lights on (per member of group using the room)	10
leaving heat on too high (per member of group using the room)	10
leaving most food waste at a meal (per person at the table)	5

•• A list of the permits with their costs, plus the fines with their costs, should be posted in the registration area, the dining room and in the sleeping rooms.

•• Have the participants bring the large envelope they received beforehand with them to registration. It should contain all of the preliminary items for the programme. You can collect these at this point (after the participants have removed their Guidebooks and chequebooks), then pass them out again at the end when you collect their pouches. (You can also remove the Congratulations cards and invitations afterwards and reuse them with another group.)

•• Since some groups won't have gone on the site tour yet, there should be a site map or instructions posted to show them how to get to their sleeping areas.

•• The reason for the three-way rotation between registration, lunch and the site tour is to keep registration from bogging down with too many people trying to go through at once. If you have a small group, you may not need to have a rotation.

•• An alternative for the name tags is to have large name cards attached to the pouches.

Permits

•• The permits are purchased for each day — at registration for day one, at Lifestyle Analysis in the evening of the first day for day two, and at Lifestyle Analysis in the evening of the second day for day three. Each time they are purchased, they are recorded on the appropriate page in the Ledger, and the amount they cost is entered into the chequebook and the cheque account is balanced.

•• Each person gets a permit card at registration for use throughout the three days. There are three spaces after each permit choice on the card. A different colour SOL stamp is used each day to show which permits were purchased for that day. Everyone must wear a permit card and a fine card at all times, including all leaders — secretaries, kitchen staff, maintenance people, parents, etc. The leader and others who are on-site when the participants arrive should already be wearing their cards. Teachers and parents can get their permits at registration too. Each leader should also have a punch and be on the lookout for violations.

•• The permits need to be enforced constantly. Sleeping areas should be checked periodically for lights left on, bathrooms/toilets checked for water violations and so on. Much of this can be done when you are in an area for other things rather than going out on patrol.

•• A public example of a fine should be included at the evening meal on the first day. Have a staff member use a paper napkin without the proper permit. Let another staff member catch and fine the individual. At the next meal have the person use a cloth napkin and point that out to everyone.

•• Whenever possible provide options and alternatives. If you have composting or pit toilets, let the participants use them rather than buying a permit for flushing toilets. Have a supply of cloth napkins in addition to paper napkins available. Some permits, however, will need to be required for everyone —brushing teeth, washing hands, flushing toilets (if there aren't any composting or pit toilets available).

•• Of course, there will be items not covered by the permits or situations the fine schedule doesn't include. Be sure to let the participants know that if something wastes energy or materials they might be fined for it even if it isn't listed as a fine. You will also need to be flexible in responding to ways the participants come up with for using less or not buying a permit — like sharing something in order to use fewer materials.

Permits	**Cost**
brushing teeth	5
flushing toilet	10
showering — up to 5 minutes	15
showering — 5 -10 minutes (or bathing)	30
using electric hair dryer	30
drinking water	5
washing hands	5
shaving with water	5
using disposable shaver	30
using electric shaver	30
wearing clothes (all cotton/plant material)	5
wearing clothes (wool)	10
wearing clothes (some natural, some synthetic material)	20
wearing clothes (all synthetic material)	30
wearing make-up	15
using paper towel	10
using paper napkin	10
wearing watch (hand wound)	5
wearing watch (battery)	25
wearing jewelry	15
using curling iron	30
using flashlight	30
using other electric appliances (each)	30

Fines	**Cost**
doing anything without a permit	2 x cost of permit
leaving water running	10
leaving lights on (per member of group using the room)	10
having heat on too high (per member of group using the room)	10
leaving most food waste at a meal (per person at the table)	5

Solarians

•• Major Branches of The Institute for Earth Education will offer discounts on t-shirts, soft tools, *The Earth Speaks*, etc. in exchange for leftover Solarians. Contact other institutions in your area (parks, nature centres, zoos, etc.) and ask them to do the same (on admissions, gifts, special experiences, etc.). This is a great way to tie in some of your local environmental centres and organizations, and it encourages the participants to venture farther afield.

•• Ask the participants to bring in a natural treasure when they come to the site. These can be displayed on a special gifting table throughout the three days. After the closing of the Commencement, participants can choose an item from the table to take with them, those with the most Solarians choosing first. (Salt this collection with specific treasures collected by the staff, parents, volunteers, etc.)

⊕ CONCEPTUAL ENCOUNTERS ⊕
(LEARNING ECOLOGICAL PRINCIPLES)

Conceptual Encounters are highly participatory and stimulating ecological learning experiences. We call them encounters because meeting them (both in their content and methods) represents an unexpected adventure for the participants. Designed for a classroom group of 20 to 30 students, they originated in **Sunship Earth**™ where they were called "Interpretive Encounters." While the "Concept Paths" in the Sunship Earth programme focus on building several concepts through a series of short activity stations set up along a trail, the Conceptual Encounters focus on building just one concept over a longer block of time. Most encounters take from one to two hours to complete.

Conceptual Encounters II is a set of the four concept activities used in the SUNSHIP III programme. Each activity includes a write-up in a "you are there" format, with much more detail than the description in this book. Also included are illustrations, leadership and prop notes, plus masters.

Conceptual Encounters II is vital for anyone setting up and running the SUNSHIP III programme but is also available to those wishing to use the activities in their own "homegrown" earth education programmes.

Conceptual Encounters are designed to meet the following criteria:

⊕ Focus upon developing a deeper understanding of one ecological concept

⊕ Emphasize peer-to-peer interactions in the learning process

⊕ Utilize a problem-solving story line

⊕ Involve ongoing roles for the participants

⊕ Require the leader to set up and direct the overall activity

A NEW KIND OF FILING SYSTEM

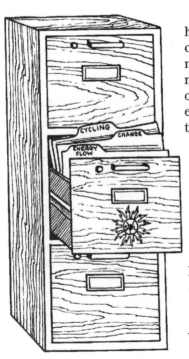

Imagine for a moment that the human brain is a gigantic filing cabinet crammed with a great number of folders. In the past, nature educators (and sadly, most of our so-called environmental educators today) spent much of their time and energy trying to label and insert filing folders in those drawers for all of the thousands upon thousands of life's pieces. This atomistic and reductionist approach has resulted, for the average person, in a great number of mostly empty folders topped with faded and tattered labels and jammed together in no apparent order.

We want to start over. We want to build and label fewer, more fluid folders that focus on the processes and places of life instead of its pieces. And we want to continue fattening up these folders both at home and school with lots of examples that relate to the participants' daily lives. In short, we want to reorganize the traditional filing system, but we also want our folders to represent function instead of form, flow instead of fossil.

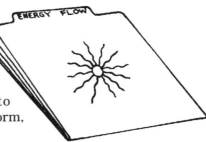

Conceptual Encounters are based upon the I-A-A Learning Model outlined in **Sunship Earth**:

I = Informing
(imparting knowledge about a natural process or place)

A = Assimilating
(making the abstract concrete through actual physical engagement)

A = Applying
(reinforcing the intended outcome by transferring the understanding to the natural setting)

Or, to put it more simply: the learners take something in, do something with it, then use it.

Conceptual Encounters either have the informing level built into the activity or utilize some other material to get this portion of the learning model across. For example, it could be something the participants read, something they view or something they listen to. In SUNSHIP III the participant's Guidebook contains important informing paragraphs for each of the four ecological understandings that the programme is based upon: energy flow, cycling, interrelationships and change. These inputs represent an important part of the overall learning model. * In the Guidebook there is also an application task after each of the concept activities. This task requires that the participants do something with what they have assimilated. It makes sure that we are getting "minds-on" as well as "hands-on" engagement.

Please note that in SUNSHIP III we have based our concept activities on the assumption that most youngsters at this age will have been introduced already to these ecological processes in their schooling.

"SOLARVILLE"
(PREVIEW)

(The four concept-building activities in SUNSHIP III are described only briefly in this book. A more complete description, along with notes, prop lists and duplication masters, is available in the Conceptual Encounters II binder available from The Institute for Earth Education.)

The true cost of a trip to a pizza joint becomes clearer on a visit to "Mario's Pizza Parlour" in "Solarville". Actually, the trip begins 150 million kilometres away, where each group of three participants receives sunlight energy in the form of 100,000 Solarians from the sun. On the way to Solarville, they'll see what happens to this sunlight energy and how it gets into the food they eat. Of course, they will lose a considerable amount of that Solarian energy along the way, but if they are lucky, they should have enough left to buy a pizza.

They head off down the sunlight trail, passing Mercury and Venus, and arrive at the entrance to the Earth's atmosphere, announced by a large welcoming sign. Unfortunately, half of the energy that reaches the earth is absorbed or reflected by the atmosphere, so it will cost them 50,000 Solarians to go on.

The next stop is an illustration of a plant, the Sunlight-Eater Station. Here they are in for a rude surprise. 95% of the sun energy that strikes the Earth is either not usable by plants or lands where there are no plants, so they have to give up 95% of their Solarians first. They slip the remaining 2,500 Solarians into the plant's "mouth" and go to the back of the sign to find they only get 250 back. Plants use up 90% of the energy they capture to grow, so only 10% is left over to become a part of the participants' long-sought pizza.

Off they go again, only to be confronted a bit farther on by a sign with a large cow's mouth extended hungrily. Plant-Eaters need energy too, so in go their remaining 250 Solarians, and again, 90% are lost. Our hungry participants are down now to just 25 Solarians. Finally, at the Meat-Eater Station, a human mouth, they find to their relief that they get to keep all 25 Solarians, since they are indeed humans.

At last they reach Solarville (with its intriguing slogan: "Where the flow of sunlight energy is not taken for granted") and meet Mario, the pizza man. Mario is delighted to make them pizzas but points out that in Solarville the cost of the pizza will depend on how much food chain energy it took to produce the ingredients.

A pizza topped with vegetables is cheaper than one with pepperoni because pepperoni comes from a longer food chain. The groups choose their pizzas from the menus and pay for them, but Mario has some more bad news to relay.

Because the ingredients must be grown, transported, processed, packaged and baked, and all of those things take energy as well, there are some hidden costs to their pizzas. The participants remove a red-checked strip from their menu to reveal the hidden costs of the pizza they have chosen. Those hidden costs must be paid for with fossil fuel energy, so Mario sends them off to the "First Fossil Fuel Reserve Bank" to cash some cheques for fossil fuel Solarians.

The bank teller is willing to help, but first explains that the reserves in the bank took millions of years to accumulate, so we must be careful about how much we choose to withdraw. Not only that, burning fossil fuels adds pollution to our air and water. As a result, some groups decide to change their pizza orders to use fewer fossil fuel Solarians, but the bank teller dips into the reserves to cash every group's cheques. The participants pay Mario for the fossil fuel costs of their pizzas, and he goes off to prepare dinner.

At the evening meal, the groups enjoy their pizzas and get a special treat when Mama Nature (Mario dressed up as his mother) pays them a visit and passes out kisses (chocolate ones) to one and all. Of course, the less energy used the more "kisses" Mama Nature bestows on a group.

ENERGY FLOW

Sunlight energy streams through space to bathe the surface of this planet each day. Green plants are the only living things which can capture this sunlight. Through the process of photosynthesis they package the sun's energy into molecules of sugar which build leaves, roots, seeds and other plant tissues.

As animals eat and digest plants, they open these packages of sunlight energy and use the energy to build their own tissues. And the energy travels even farther when another animal (such as a hawk) eats the plant-eater (such as a rabbit). This path of energy flow, from the sun to plants to plant-eaters to animal-eaters, is called a food chain.

As energy moves along the food chain, much of it is used up and lost. Before they are eaten, plants use up much of their energy just to grow, and animals use up a great deal of sunlight energy as they move around. Because of this energy loss, there is less energy available farther up the food chain, so in most food chains, there are many plants, fewer plant-eaters and even fewer animal-eaters.

Millions of years ago, some of the sunlight energy captured by plants was buried underground when the plants died. Over time, this stored sunlight energy turned into coal, oil and natural gas, the "fossil" fuels we use today to power our automobiles, heat our homes, provide our electricity and so on. The supplies of fossil fuels are limited and are being depleted. In addition, our use of fossil fuels creates other problems, from air pollution to acid rain to global warming.

"MAGIC SPOTS"
(ENJOYING SOLITUDE)

A teenage boy sits alone, leaning comfortably against a tree trunk. He is by himself but knows that his friends and leaders are not far away. There is no sound of human voices, no noise but the murmuring of the branches in the wind, some birds singing, a stream meandering on its way, a single leaf scuttling along the ground. He comes to this special spot he has chosen in the forest to pause and reflect, to ponder and dream. He looks up to see the pattern of the branches of "his" tree against the sky, leans back to feel its bark against his skin, reaches out to touch the soil at its roots. This is his Magic Spot.

A Magic Spot is a very special place to be alone and bask in the richness of nature. On each day of the Commencement Exercises each participant selects and spends time in a Magic Spot in a different natural community or "Section Of Life." Everyone then has an opportunity to experience three different communities of life during the programme.

On the first day, the leader gathers the group in a circle to explain the idea of Magic Spots. Participants are cautioned to be very careful about selecting one small spot from so many possibilities. "Your spot should be out of sight and hearing from other spots if possible," suggests the leader. "It should be a place where you can sit comfortably, maybe with a tree or rock to lean against. But most importantly, it should be a place where you can feel like you are alone."

The Ledger contains a section titled "my perceptions" that has inputs to read as well as pages where participants can record their thoughts about what they are experiencing as they go

through the Commencement Exercises. Part of each Magic Spot time is spent reflecting on their changing perceptions, but part is also spent getting in tune with the flow of life — becoming familiar with that particular spot, listening to its sounds, taking in its colours — that is, after all, the overriding goal of Magic Spots.

At the end of Magic Spot time, the leader blows a conch shell or hoots like an owl to signal the time to return to the circle. Several participants share some of their Magic Spot experience with the group. Amid the excitement of the high energy Commencement Exercises, everyone has had a chance to slow down and personally get to know one particular place in one of the earth's incredible natural communities.

NOTES, CUES AND PROPS

•• The success of Magic Spots depends to a large extent on the leader's preparation. The stage should be set carefully. In order to make the spot truly "magical", there are three main points to include:

> **Alone** — each Magic Spot should be isolated enough that the person using it can feel like he or she is the only one around; in a fairly small area emphasize the importance of finding a spot where other people are not visible.

> **Sitting** — sitting still rather than wandering, sitting upright rather than lying down.

> **Quiet** — this doesn't mean just not talking but also not crunching sticks, crumpling leaves, whistling, tossing rocks into water, etc. — trying to be silent.

•• Magic Spots encourage direct contact with the natural world. Simply being outside is not enough. Everyone should sit on the ground. If the ground is wet, muddy or snowy, provide "sit-upons" (squares of ensolite pads or carpet, for example) or have participants sit on their rain gear.

•• The size of a Magic Spot group depends on how many participants you have, how many different natural communities, the size and type of natural area and so on. Generally, it is better to have a fairly small number of participants in each group. It makes the introduction, Magic Spot selection and sharing easier.

•• During the introduction a leader can begin with a short reading from **The Earth Speaks**.

•• As in so many things, the example the leaders set is crucial. Having leaders in Magic Spots themselves is more effective than having them patrol among others' Magic Spots.

⊕ SHARING CIRCLES ⊕
(PROCESSING IDEAS)

Sharing Circles are a crucial element in the SUNSHIP III programme, from helping with the preparation beforehand, to processing what is happening enroute, to keeping the Quest on track back at home and school.

Each Sharing Circle is made up of ten to fifteen students carefully chosen ahead of time by the teacher. (A mix of different personalities and abilities is preferred.) The groups meet first

before their visit to the centre to help each other prepare for the Readiness Check and, if necessary, to prepare for a second one.

Each day at the site, there is time scheduled for Sharing Circles. A staff member (Guide) heads up each session. The meeting is spent talking about what has been happening in the programme, what the participants think about what they are experiencing and what must be done to prepare for the Quest that lies ahead. To prevent a few highly verbal participants from dominating the interaction, a special "message stick" is passed from person to person at some point during most Sharing Circles. No one else in the group can speak except the person holding the stick. However, when someone lies the stick down instead of passing it along, it is an invitation to respond to the point raised so anyone can join in (except the person who laid it down). Although the leaders are bound by the same rules, they also serve as timekeepers, setting the maximum length of time any one person can control the stick in each session (usually 1, 3, 5 or 7 minutes).

Back at school, the Sharing Circles occur at a regular meeting time so the participants can talk about how they are doing on their Quests, sharing experiences and suggestions. Naturally, the time spent together at the SUNSHIP III site is very important for setting the tone and purpose for the Sharing Circles. The way the group interacts afterwards is in large part determined by how they started working together at the site.

NOTES, CUES AND PROPS

•• Message sticks are 30 cm (foot long), forked branches (like the Y part of the SOL symbol).

•• Although passing the message stick may not be necessary during each Sharing Circle at the site, it should be done a couple of times to set the stage for how it will work when the group returns.

⊕ LIFESTYLE ANALYSIS ⊕
(SEEING CHOICES)

Each evening the participants record in their Ledgers the Solarians they spent that day, then buy permits for the next day. This is preceded on the first evening by a film about how energy is used in the production of food and on the second evening by a skit on a typical day in the life of a teenager.

First Evening — Film

All of the participants gather to watch a film that deals with perceptions — in this case, revealing more about the energy used in the production of their food. At the end of the film, Sharing Circles meet to talk about the film and about how they spent their first day. Then the participants record the Solarians they spent that day (in their Ledgers) and buy the permits they will need for the second day.

Second Evening — Skit

"BILLY'S DAY"
(HABITS AND ROUTINES)

All the participants gather to watch a skit that portrays a day in the life of someone their own age. The focus is on individual routines and habits and how we settle into these patterns (which are often environmentally unsound) without giving them much thought.

"Billy", a staff member, walks to the front of the group, lies down on a table with a pillow under his head and begins to snore gently.

Gael, the narrator, moves to the front, finger on lips to signal that everyone should be quiet, then addresses the group:

"Shhh... Billy's asleep. Pretty soon he will wake up, and you'll be able to watch a somewhat shortened but typical day in his life. Pay attention to how his daily routines are made up of a lot of habits that he probably never analyzed. If you see something that Billy is doing that is wasting energy or materials, for example, or if you have a suggestion for some way he could use less, just raise your hand. I'll 'freeze' Billy (every once in a while), and we'll quickly talk about your ideas and note them on the chalkboard. Then we'll let him get on with his day. Let's begin."

(The narrator talks Billy through his day, describing his actions or giving voice to his thoughts. Billy is silent, using movement and just a few simple props to show what is being described.)

"Billy always wakes up to his radio alarm playing KIX, his favourite station."

Billy puts the pillow over his head and ignores the radio.

"Forget it, Billy, mum is on the warpath: 'Get out of that bed; shake a leg!'"

Billy groans, sits up, rubs his eyes.

"Hmmm... it's dark in here with the curtains drawn."

He switches on the light.

"That's better."

"Should get dressed, I suppose. Might just see what's on the telly first though."

Billy switches the set on and slumps down in a chair in front of it.

"Boring 'Ghostbusters' again; seen them a million times. Where's the Walkman?"

He puts on a Walkman and brightens up perceptibly, jigging around in time to the music as he continues to gaze at the television.

"Time's getting along, Billy. Better get into the bathroom before mum comes storming up here."

Billy leaves the room, moving to the other side of the table.

"Bit dark in here, too."

He switches on a light.

"How about a shower; might wake you up a bit."

Billy turns on the tap and gingerly sticks his hand out to test the water — too cold! After a bit, he gets the right adjustment. He then proceeds to get undressed: removes his pyjamas, stops to admire his muscles in the mirror and finally steps into the shower.

"Hey, don't forget to turn up the radio."

Billy scrubs in the shower.

"That feels good. Don't forget to work your back though. Where's the shampoo?"

He squeezes on a very liberal amount and rubs it in, then rinses.

"Now for conditioner; got to look after your hair."

Once again he squeezes out a lot and repeats the process. He then slumps forward, allowing water to run down his back. Obviously, he's just enjoying the water.

"Come on, Billy, out you go. Time to dry off."

He towels himself dry, then puts on underwear and track pants. He stops to sniff his arm pits.

"Oh, yes, deodorant. Never know who you'll meet after phys ed today. Ahhh... love those chemicals."

He sprays far more than needed under his arms, stops to consider, then sprays some more.

"Better finish getting dressed, Billy."

"Now, time to polish the old fangs."

Billy bares his teeth, peering closely into the mirror. He turns on the tap, fits his toothbrush into the electric holder and, after applying a lot of toothpaste, switches it on.

"Now, what's left. Oh, yes, your hair. Got to get it just right. Bit of mousse first, hey?"

He squirts a large amount of mousse from a bottle and rubs it in. He then proceeds to comb his hair, finishing up by forming a large spike on top of his head.

"Look's great!" Billy turns his head to admire himself in the mirror. **"Still a bit damp. The hair dryer should finish it off."**

Billy turns on a hair dryer and aims it at his head.

"Come on, Billy; time for breakfast. You have to get to school today. Hey, remember your Walkman."

Billy walks to the other end of the table, which now becomes the kitchen.

"Mum never puts the blinds up."

He switches on the light.

"What to eat? Check the fridge."

Billy opens the refrigerator door and stands undecided for a long time gazing into it.

"Oh, yeah. Milk."

He takes out the milk, leaving the refrigerator door open.

"May as well put on the kettle for a cup of tea."

Billy picks up the kettle, turns on the tap and leaves it there, obviously filling the kettle completely. He switches it on and returns to the table jigging in time to the music on his Walkman.

"How about some Wheatos?"

Billy pours out a very large bowl full. He adds milk and begins to eat while continuing to nod in time to the music.

"Billy, Billy! Kettle's boiling!"

Billy leaps to his feet to turn off the kettle. He jiggles his tea bag as he returns to the table and starts eating again.

"Hey, Billy, look at the time. Mum's out in the car blowing the horn. Time to go to school."

Billy rushes from the room, leaving his breakfast on the table and collapses in the car.

"Good old mum.   Just as well she's here to drive you."

Billy sits on a chair and is driven to school.

"Out you go.   The bell's rung and school's already started."

Billy takes the chair across the room with him and sits down in it.

**"Creative writing this morning: 'A Day in the Life of a Slug'.
Billy's finding it a bit hard to find the right beginning."**

*He writes a few words, crumples up the paper and begins again
on a new sheet.*

**"Saved by the bell.   Lunch at last.   Let's check out the
canteen."**

*Billy walks over and stands at a pretend counter, points to this
and that, and pays his money.*

"What does Billy have for lunch? Oh, a meat pie (he unwraps the pie from the plastic wrapper and throws the wrapper into a bin)... and tomato sauce (he opens the small sauce container, adds it to the pie and throws that container in the bin)... and a can of soda (he opens the can, drinks it and throws the empty can in the bin too).

"Bell's ringing. Back into the old prison. Billy's hard at work again."

He sits staring into space.

"School's over. Good old mum, waiting outside with the car as usual."

He sits in the chair.

"Now, have to relax after a hard day. Try the telly."

He switches on the set, gazes blankly for a few moments, then wanders off.

"Dumb cartoons, as usual. How about a computer game? Billy's great at those. He spends hours practising and gets top scores."

Billy switches on the computer and begins to play avidly.

"Where does the time go? Mum and dad are at the club, so it's up to you to get your own dinner. What will it be?"

Billy wanders into the kitchen, turns on a light and opens the fridge. After a bit he opens the freezer door, leaving the fridge door open in the process.

"Great, there's a frozen pizza! Pop it in the microwave."

He unwraps the pizza, puts it into the microwave and throws the wrapper into a bin. He then puts on his headphones.

"May as well have a bit of music while you wait for it to heat."

Pause.

"Hey, Billy! Take off the headphones and listen. Your pizza's ready."

He runs to the microwave, takes out the pizza and eats it.

"Gee, it's been a long day. Too tired for homework tonight. You can do it in the morning."

Billy yawns and stumbles off to bed. He lies down on the table with the pillow under his head, clicking his fingers and nodding his head to the music till he falls asleep.

"Shh... Billy's asleep."

At the end of the skit, it is done a second time putting in the changes suggested by the group. When it is finished, after a big round of applause, the participants break off into Sharing Circles to talk about the skit, things they do on their "typical" days, record the Solarians they spent and buy permits for the third day.

NOTES, CUES AND PROPS

"Billy's Day"

•• The person playing Billy should wear a full dancer's body stocking (with a female staff member, "Billy" can easily become "Sally").

•• Use few props - a table, chair, pillow, shampoo, conditioner, spray deodorant, mousse, gel, a box of cereal, etc.

•• During the stop-action, when Billy freezes, a teacher or staff member should write down the suggestions on a chalkboard.

•• If possible, add piped in sound effects (but they must be flawlessly executed or the hilarity of late or mismatched sounds will overwhelm the message).

Recording Solarians

•• There is a separate page in the Ledger for recording the Solarians spent each day. On the first evening, the participants start off by writing in the amount of Solarians they spent on permits that day, plus any Solarians they were fined. Next they analyze permits that weren't really needed and note ways to do without some of them. Each person then selects permits for the next day, writes them down in the Ledger for Day 2 and writes a cheque for the amount needed for those permits. Guides take the cheques and help balance the chequebooks.

Daily Needs Ledger - Day 1
Permits Purchased

Permit	Cost
brushing teeth	5
flushing toilet	10
washing hands	5
drinking water	5
showering - up to 5 minutes	15
wearing clothes (natural & synthetic)	20
wearing watch (pottery)	25
using flashlight	30
Total Permit Cost	115

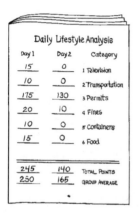

Daily Lifestyle Analysis

Day 1	Day 2	Category
15	0	1 Television
10	0	2 Transportation
175	130	3 Permits
20	10	4 Fines
10	0	5 Containers
15	0	6 Food
245	140	TOTAL POINTS
250	165	GROUP AVERAGE

•• Another page in the Ledger (the Daily Lifestyle Analysis page) lists several categories of things that use energy and materials. It has a column for Day 1 and a column for Day 2. On the evening of Day 1, the participants record numbers in the first column to reflect the energy and materials used that day. On the second evening they do the same in the next column. The goal is to get the second day's total to be less than the first day's. A Guide helps them fill out the page, explaining each entry and how to score it using the suggestions below. The numbers are rather arbitrary and are meant to serve as a focal point for talking things over rather than being important in themselves.

•• During the final Sharing Circle time on the third morning, before the group talks about the Quest, a few minutes are taken to record the Solarians spent that day after reviewing the Lifestyle Analysis chart.

LIFESTYLE ANALYSIS

Catagory   **Points**

1. Television (if you watched it today)   15

2. Transportation
   (if you — walked to school   0
            — rode a bicycle   5
            — rode a school bus   10
            — rode in a car   25

3. Permits
   (note the total Solarians you spent on permits today)

4. Fines (if you were fined today, write the amount)

5. Containers (add 5 points for each metal can, glass bottle,
   or jar, or plastic container you "threw away" today)

6. Food (if you ate overly packaged, highly processed
   food today, add 5 points for each different food item)

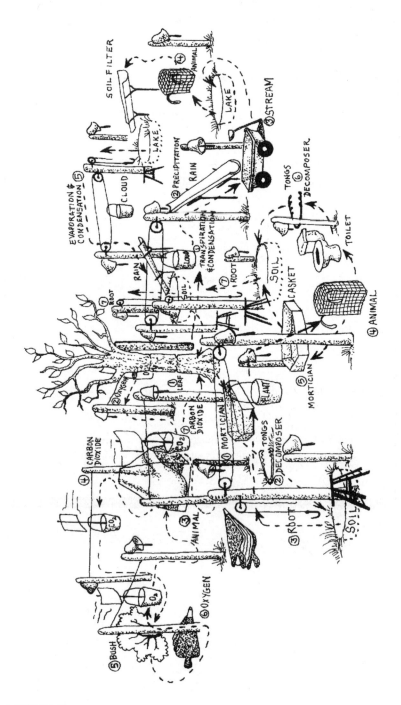

"CYCLE FACTORY"
(PREVIEW)

All living things on SUNSHIP III are supported and nourished by the soil, air and water on board. Because these materials are in limited supply, they must be used over and over. In The Cycle Factory, participants experience first-hand this process of renewal by physically moving the materials through their cycles.

The factory itself resembles a bizarre Rube Goldberg contraption of pulleys and posts, bellows and bells, chutes and ladders. In the centre is a large, rather weird looking tree that you can see into. Arrayed around the tree are three "assembly loops" (since cycles aren't lines but "circles in time"). Donning colour-coded hard hats (brown for soil, light blue for air and dark blue for water), the factory workers report to their first shifts. Their mission: to operate the cycles and provide enough materials to "grow" their tree (materials represented by painted whiffle or cosum balls).

Foremen (and -women) meet each group and explain the complete cycle and each person's role in it. In the air cycle, light blue balls move between plants and animals on their way to the tree. Some workers use bellows to blow the air molecules from animal to plant along special routes, while others take the molecules through a giant nose as the animal breathes them in and out. In the water cycle, dark blue balls travel down a "stream" in a wagon, "rain" into a "lake" by rolling down a chute, or get pulled up out of the ground on a hook by "plants", all on their way to the tree. In the soil cycle (brown balls), "morticians" move dead plants and animals to "decomposers" who transfer them to the soil, while "plants" pull up soil nutrients and hand them to "animals" who eat them, before dying or releasing the nutrients as "waste"; either way the soil nutrients are returned to the tree by way of other "decomposers".

The workers have phrases to call out as they do their jobs ("returning waste nutrients to the soil", "stream flowing", "oxygen in, food into energy, carbon dioxide out") and bells to ring each time they move some material along.

When the groups know their jobs, the supervisor calls for work to begin, and the scene becomes one of organized chaos. As the sound of bells and calling out of actions announces the movement of molecules around the cycles, the trunk of the tree begins to fill with materials. The supervisor keeps everyone at work by shouting out encouragement, and when the tree is full, signals a rest break.

While everyone takes a breather, the supervisor adds another section to the tree. It has grown and needs additional nutrients, air and water. Everyone moves to a new shift, and after practising the new cycles, work begins again. Since these systems are cycles, balls are also taken periodically from the tree as it loses nutrients when its leaves fall and gives off oxygen as it makes food. The workers must move quickly now to replenish the tree faster than it loses its material. When they fill the second section, a water break is signaled.

When everyone has been trained to work on their third shift and another section has been added to the tree, the sudden appearance of some black balls concerns the participants. These balls represent the pollutants and poisons that people add to the water, air and soil. Because materials move in great cycles, the poisons travel with them, and if too many poisons build up in our tree, it will become sick and die.

Work begins on the third shift and some black balls begin showing up in the tree. However, the factory workers push on diligently, and eventually the tree is completed. The workers finish by learning some things they can do to release fewer poisons into the cycles, then receive Solarian paycheques for their hard work on the assembly "loops".

CYCLING

The building materials of life are hydrogen, carbon, oxygen, nitrogen, phosphorus and sulphur. There is a limited supply of these materials on earth, and they must be reused by all living things. They are constantly being taken up from and returned to the air, soil and waters of the earth.

The soil is the great nourisher of plants, providing the nutrients which they need to grow. The soil would be useless if there was no way of getting these nutrients back after they had been taken out by the plants. But the soil is constantly being replenished, for there are millions of bacteria in each handful of soil that break down waste matter and dead animals and plants and return the nutrients which these things contain back to the soil. And so the cycling of soil re-uses the building materials of life.

Water on the earth is moved by the heat of the sun through a great water cycle. Water evaporates from the rivers, lakes and oceans of the world and rises up into the sky where it condenses into clouds. From here the water falls back to the earth in the form of rain, snow, sleet or hail, only to flow once again into the rivers, lakes and oceans. Occasionally, the water takes a detour through a living thing. Evaporation and the filtering action of the soil are important purifiers in the cycling of water.

Parts of the air are also used over and over. With every breath animals of the earth exhale carbon dioxide. Plants use this carbon dioxide from the air when they make sugars in their leaves; and a byproduct of this sugar-making process is oxygen, which the plants release into the air. Thus the cycling of air provides for the exchange of essential needs of life for both plants and animals.

"MUSEUM PROJECT"
(PREVIEW)

A long-forgotten museum exhibit chronicling the past of a natural area becomes the vehicle for discovering how all things change over time on SUNSHIP III.

A collection of half a dozen dusty old crates, containing natural items that represent what a particular area has been like at various times in the past, has been dug out for the participants, along with the explanation that the local museum would like their help in figuring out what all this stuff means. After each small group opens a crate, they dig through the old excelsior to find bits and pieces that indicate the site, wherever it was, was once a desert, an ocean, a lake, a meadow and a marsh. The items have museum tags and code numbers (since they came from an old exhibit), but each crate contains one item that doesn't seem to belong with the others. The desert crate, for example, along with vials of sand and cactus spines, holds a fossil seashell. These items end up helping the group figure out which communities are the oldest and the sequence of their development.

The participants work together to figure out which crate represents the oldest community and label a chalkboard with the level in the ground where each would be found. The ocean is the oldest, so it goes on the bottom. Each succeeding community (desert, lake, marsh, meadow) goes above it. Some of the changes, from ocean to desert for example, took millions of years to happen. Others, like the transition from marsh to meadow, happened much faster by comparison.

As the participants lay the items from each community out in order on a table, another staff member at the centre wanders in and recognizes the items as being the kind that would have been found at the centre itself long ago. She concludes that they must be from an exhibit she had seen pictures of, one detailing the geological history of this very same area.

Excitedly, the group tries to reconstruct that exhibit, using a fibreboard backdrop and other props which their leader just happens to have on hand. They also gather items outside from the forest this area has now become, so they can add that part of the area's history to their exhibit. On cards, they write descriptive captions for these new items.

As they work, the staff member comes in again to check on their progress. She asks if they are sure they got everything from the museum, because the graphics and explanatory stuff seem to be missing. In a previously "undiscovered" crate, they find signs, notebook pages, labels and letters to complete the exhibit, including the overall title: "Everything Changes Over Time".

When they complete their "lost" exhibit, the leader takes a picture to send to the local museum and gives everyone a free pass for it as a reward for all their hard work.

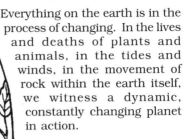

CHANGE

Everything on the earth is in the process of changing. In the lives and deaths of plants and animals, in the tides and winds, in the movement of rock within the earth itself, we witness a dynamic, constantly changing planet in action.

Many changes on earth occur so slowly that we cannot see them happening. The growth and movement of continents, glaciers, mountains and valleys takes thousands of years. These and many other major earth changes require enormous amounts of time as their most important ingredient.

Certain changes in natural communities happen in a series of distinct stages. One such change is the succession of a new kind of plant which is able to live in the shade or soil built up by another kind of plant. A series of such stages can, over a long period of time, cover bare rock with forest, and even though we could not witness the whole process in one lifetime, we can often see one or two of the stages of the change.

Every living thing has a built-in strategy which enables it to survive — a strategy to protect itself, get food and water, and reproduce. These strategies may take the form of special features — such as the webbed feet of a duck, the pinchers of a crab or the thorns of a shrub. In addition, the behaviour of an individual may also be part of this strategy. Some trees lose their leaves in the winter, birds often fly to warmer climates, and many animals are active at night when they can be protected by darkness. Each living thing has a unique combination of features and behaviour patterns to solve its problems of living.

However, life is not static. Over time, life forms emerge with better fitting features and behaviour patterns and replace those which are less prepared. This process of adaptation is the cutting edge for the success of life on earth: those best fit survive in the end because they live to reproduce and pass along their improved strategies.

⊕ Discovery Parties ⊕
(Instilling Wonder)

Free wheeling and adventuresome, Discovery Parties are activities that encourage participants to discover for themselves some of the marvelous things that share the earth with us. They are light in tone, offering, in a sense, an excuse to poke around, explore and share. There is just enough structure to hold a group together, enough freedom to encourage individual "finds". This popular earth education vehicle is similar to a natural history walk or talk in that a knowledgeable leader can provide appropriate "fun facts", but different in that the participants make the discoveries, while the leaders may only respond briefly to what they come up with. It takes a lot of restraint at times to hold back, but please remember that in earth education the learners are supposed to be the stars.

Discovery Parties are designed to meet the following criteria:

⊕ focus on building a sense of wonder and place

⊕ include tasks for encouraging personal exploration and making individual "finds"

⊕ emphasize making firsthand contact with natural places and things

⊕ utilize the participants in deciding moment to moment where to go and what to do within a specific setting

⊕ involve opportunities for leaders to share both wonder and knowledge

⊕ require the leader to set the stage, then respond more than initiate

"Objet Trouvé"
(FINDING BEAUTY)

Part One

The participants enter a curtained-off section of a room that contains a number of tan pedestals of various heights. A signboard on an easel out front announced the opening of an exhibit of lost treasures, but inside only a few of the pedestals have objects on them; most are empty. Actually, the main attraction is Nancy. Dressed in an earth-stained smock with a colourful scarf wrapped around her head and bits of plants and stuff sticking out of her pockets, she runs frantically from one pedestal to the next, moving objects and making exclamations of both delight and frustration. She soon notices the group and calls out in a heavy accent, "Ah, excuse me. I have a show opening today, but I have only a few treasures to exhibit. The rest were lost in shipment. I don't know what to do."

"Can we help?" responds one of the participants.

"Well, this is an exhibit of natural treasures from some of the most incredible Sections Of Life on Earth," Nancy explains. "This part of the exhibit is the forest section," she continues as she shows off a few treasures already in place: a small intricately twisted piece of vine, a chunk of wood with a mottled fungus growing on it and several coloured leaves painstakingly arranged under a nut. Each has a simple title on a small card stapled to the side of its pedestal.

"These beauties were found in some of the most inaccessible places on Earth. You know, it's said beauty is in the eye of the beholder, but in this case I think it's in the hand of the discoverer as well. And the more arduous the journey in finding the object, the better the discoverer can appreciate the beauty I was seeking for my exhibit. Let me explain: to really appreciate natural beauty

you have to push beyond the comfort of your nice paths, your special boots and clothing, and meet it on its own terms, in its own setting. You have to feel what it feels, and see the world from its vantage point. These may look like commonplace objects, but they were formed by those who experienced their reality."

"Hey, we've been doing something like that at our Magic Spots," someone volunteers.

"I don't know how. Look at you: you don't look like you've ever wallowed in the world. You're too clean — all swathed in synthetics — there's not a smudge of good earth on any of you! Do you think you could really get out there and immerse yourself in one of the natural communities here? And do it in such a way that you would be able to feel what the things living there feel?"

"Sure, we can handle that," Kazu responds.

"You can't find treasures like this just by walking along a path," Nancy clarifies. "You have to crawl and climb, slog and slide, wiggle and worm your way into an area. Only then can you prepare yourself adequately to experience its place in the world. Today, the best natural treasures are often discovered in some out of the way corner where no one thought to look. Let me just tell you what I went through personally to find this one piece..."

After she tells its story, Nancy moves among the pedestals explaining how different people discovered a few of the other items: "Fran wormed his way into this amazing thicket to find this little beauty. And Jeff spent an hour lying among the reeds trying to see the world from the vantage point of this wonderful shell."

She hastens to add that these works of art are just on loan from the "real museum", that is the **S**ections **O**f **L**ife found in the natural world, and she is just arranging them in a way that will intensify a particular quality. However, the entire time she is showing off her treasures, ("Here I was trying for elemental simplicity, over there for fundamental unity, and back here to highlight an unusual metaphorical shape.") Nancy shifts back and forth from a proud artist carefully explaining the subtleties of the work and the ardor of its discoverer to a nervous exhibitor

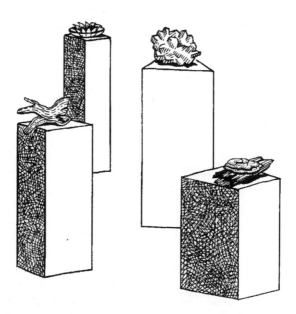

almost overcome with anxiety about the upcoming show. Finally, she slumps down on the floor, holding her head in her hands. "Oh, it's just hopeless," she cries. "I had such wonderful things for this show. They came from all over the world."

"Wait a minute. There's stuff like this right around here," one participant exclaims.

"That's right," another chimes in. "I saw some fungus like this on our tour yesterday."

"Really?...," Nancy brightens up. "If you think you could get out there and get off the beaten track, <u>really</u> getting down and dirty, maybe we could borrow some of those things to fill out my show." Gaining confidence, she adds, "In the theatre, Stanislavski said you have to improvise. So that's what we'll do with my exhibit. Improvise!"

Nancy asks the group for their help in "borrowing" natural treasures for the show and sends them out to the forest. Later, she gives a similar introduction to another group in the stream section of the gallery, and then a third for the meadow. In each case, before sending them off, she reminds them that they will only be borrowing the items from their natural communities so they should take great care in deciding what to bring back. And they must be prepared to tell the story of how they made their discovery and experienced its world.

When the first group arrives at the forest, each person searches for one special object to display. Using an enlarged section of the map they saw on their site tour, the participants mark on it the spots where they found their natural artworks. They also leave a brief note hidden in each spot explaining what they did there to immerse themselves in its world, so someone will be able to return the objects later to their proper places and have the same experience.

Everyone then returns to the gallery to finish the exhibit. Each person gets a pedestal and arranges his or her own display. Nancy mingles with the group offering suggestions and thanking everyone profusely. "Who would have ever guessed that we could find such marvelous artwork right here," she bubbles. She also gives each person a small card, for each treasure will need its own special title.

When everything is ready, Nancy invites the group to return when the other sections of the exhibit are finished so they can view the whole gallery.

Part Two

When all three groups have finished their sections of the gallery, the black, movable curtains separating the areas are taken down. Each group returns at a different time to view the entire gallery. Two uniformed guards are standing near the door. Each section of the gallery is designated with a sign suspended from the ceiling: "forest", "stream" or "meadow". And recordings of the sounds of nature fill the air with natural music.

Nancy asks everyone to mingle and enjoy the treasures. As they do, the guards wander through the gallery, not to enforce the rules but to encourage everyone to look more closely, to smell and to touch the treasures. These are unusual guards indeed. They even have hand lenses for the participants to use and small mist sprayers to help bring out the colours and smells. Where appropriate they share a few "fun facts" about the items as they make their rounds. Hosts and hostesses appear carrying trays of cheese and crackers and sparkling cider. Nancy, of course, is having the time of her life sharing all the new "discoveries" exhibited. "Can't you just feel the colour in that?" "Oh, I say, this one is just superb." "Who would've guessed a little old insect could have done that..." "Isn't this the most scintillating piece you've ever seen?"

After what seems like a brief time, the lights begin to dim, the music fades, the refreshments are carried away, and Nancy announces that the show must come to an end. She thanks them for coming and asks them to return later in the day to help with the final closing of the exhibit.

Part Three

The dividers between the sections of the gallery are back in place as all the groups return, each at a different time and to a different section than the one they helped set up. Their task is to take the treasures and return them to where they belong. Each group uses the section of the map prepared by those that originally set up the exhibit for the area. Nancy, who doubted at first that anything approaching the superlative quality of her "lost" treasures could ever be "found" at this centre, has become overly solicitous about their welfare. "Please, please be careful with these masterpieces, my dears." "Oh, you will handle them gently, won't you? I just hate to part with such pure beauty."

When an object is returned to its rightful spot, of course, the note left by its finder is waiting to let the person know that this is truly the object's home and to guide that participant into experiencing its small place in space.

NOTES, CUES AND PROPS

•• The role of the artist should be played by someone with a flair for the dramatic and a passable accent in another language. (Although Nancy may seem a bit distracted, perhaps overblown here, her vocabulary and insights should also reflect serious observation. Even though she obviously performs for the group, once again, the "hook" will be the genuine intellectual appeal she can bring to bear on commonplace objects and the sense of adventure she imparts to their discovery.)

•• The activity as described is set up for three groups of 15-20 participants. If you have a different number of groups, simply adjust the numbers of sections (natural communities) you use.

•• The examples for the natural communities given are forest, meadow and stream, but others would work just as well — desert, pond, marsh, etc. If you don't have the needed number of distinct natural communities close at hand, you should find areas with as many differences as possible — forests may have edges, openings, wet areas, hillsides, thick undergrowth, shaded places, and so on.

•• The sample objects already on the pedestals in the introduction should be carefully planned and set up. The focus should be on the simple beauty of ordinary things when they are properly shown rather than on creating elaborate decorative arrangements using many objects.

•• In French, Objet Trouvé indicates the "Lost and Found" spot.

•• Pedestals — 1 per participant, plus several for the samples. They can be made of wood or heavy cardboard and should be painted a light tan colour. There should also be a variety of sizes — from 1 to 1 1/2 meters (3-5 feet) tall, but all one shape - square, round, or triangular - is best.

•• Title cards — 1 per participant, plus several for the samples. A border should be drawn on each one.

•• Dark pencils to write on the title cards

•• 1 earth-stained smock

•• 1 multi-coloured head scarf

•• Numerous natural items (pinned or sewn on the scarf and smock, sticking out of every fold and pocket in the cloth)

•• 2 security guard uniforms

•• Hand magnifying lenses — several for each guard

•• Misting bottles and water

•• 1 sign for each section of the exhibit — forest, stream, etc.

•• Serving trays — for each host/hostess

•• Cheese, crackers, sparkling cider

•• Stemmed non-disposable glasses for the cider

•• Music — recordings of natural sounds

•• Tape player and speakers for the music

•• 1 enlarged section of the site map (for each group)

•• 1 sheet of notepaper per participant (for notes)

•• Pencils for marking the map and writing the notes

"TEMPLE OF SOL" — PART ONE
(PREVIEW)

The ruins of a strange temple, the story of an ancient people, and the deciphering of mysterious glyphs invite exploration about how all the systems of SUNSHIP III are integrated to support life, and initiate the process of helping young people take responsibility for the consequences their actions have on the earth.

On the second evening of their training, the young passengers of SUNSHIP III are led by lantern light to a spot in the forest where a tumble-down pile of rocks forms a low wall. A dozen candles placed among the rocks provide the lighting as a staff member explains about the People of SOL who lived in this area long ago. She points out a fishhook and other strange hieroglyphics carved into some of the rocks. On one large stone a bowl-shaped depression is divided into three parts. This is the SOL stone, and the entire area represents the ruins of the Temple of SOL.

In short, after a lot of research, the staff of the centre believes they have pieced together the story of what happened here. When the young people of SOL were making the transition from childhood to adulthood, they were brought to this place to hear from Earth Woman. She was never seen, but her instructions for the young people had great power, and the staff wants to share what they have deciphered of her words...

"EARTH WOMAN"
(EXPLORATION AND DISCOVERY)

"Welcome, my children. You have come to that point of your life where you have begun changing in mysterious ways. Like the green, fuzzy worm that becomes a colourful, free-spirited butterfly, you have begun your own passage between the world of children and the world of adults. This will be a difficult time in your life, for those childish ways you still cling to must die in order for your adult self to be born.

Hear my words and heed them: From this day forward, you must begin taking responsibility for your own actions and accepting the consequences of them.

Soon you will leave the comfort and security of home and family and set out on a quest seeking environmental truth, adventure and harmony. It will be the most important journey of your life. Many of your people have set off on this journey of self-discovery before you, not all of them have returned. Those who wear the symbol that you have been shown are those who have completed their quest. It is the symbol of SOL. The people who wear it will survive in this land only so long as most of them return from their journey knowing how to live responsibly on the earth.

Acting responsibly is not always easy. You will be tempted many times along the way to participate in childish things and lose sight of your goal. You must learn to see with both your head and your heart. Choose wisely at each stage of your journey for once you set out you can never go back.

Your quest will have three parts to it, corresponding to the environmental truth, adventure and harmony that you seek, and each of you will be given a small pouch containing the things you will need for discovering those three doctrines of your people.

Note well the hook you see carved into the stone at this spot. It is my mark. You must learn first on your quest how to fish for environmental truth, just as the people who live on the great waters fish for their food. Remember: environmental truth is seldom found on the surface; it is found deep within both people and places.

Inside your pouch you will find a small hook like mine to take with you on your journey. Wear it around your neck, inside your tunic, as a reminder of your task as a seeker of environmental truth. When you go to bed at night, hang your hook overhead and it will help you find that truth, for in your dreams swims a fish that lives deep within your minds. When you hook onto it and pull it up, you will see that the scales on one side of this fish say, "thou shalt", and on the other, "thou shalt not." Look closely at what you find written there for those things represent some of the most important decisions of your life. During your quest for the environmental truth you will have to choose what you will and will not do as an adult.

Hear my words and heed them, my children: The world does not exist to make you happy; you exist for the pleasure of the world.

You will also find in your pouch several natural objects. They are pieces of mother earth. During your quest you must return them to their proper homes. The map in the great stone will guide you. You can go alone or with others, but you must not let either the little voice in your mind or the voices of your companions distract you from your adventure.

Remain alert and take note of what is happening to you as you make your way into new lands. Among the people of SOL an adult is one who understands that what is seen must be measured against what is felt. So you should pay close attention to your feelings as you proceed and keep a record of your journey.

When you arrive at one of these home places, find a Magic Spot there, hang your hook nearby and hold the piece of this place in your hand. Take your time. Be patient. If you look and listen with your heart as well as your head, if you remain quiet and unafraid, if you let the sun move through the great sky undisturbed, you will hook onto the truth of this place as well.

When you have done this three times, you will have completed another vital part of your quest to take your rightful place among your people.

Hear my words, my children, and heed them: Going somewhere is good, but really being somewhere is better.

The third thing you will discover in your pouch is a wristband. It is the band of environmental harmony. You must wear it until your quest has ended. By this band you will be known as a seeker from SOL.

You must find others who wear this band and learn from them how they are trying to live in harmony with the earth. Wherever you find a circle with a line through it on your map, there you will find someone wearing a band like yours. You must seek these people out and talk with them and discover how they have found harmony between environmental truth and adventure in their lives.

Most important, you must decide as you go how you will craft your own life, for a proper life should not be like the accumulated bits and pieces that get trapped in the stagnant water behind a log in the river; it should be a free-flowing life of conscious choice.

When you have chosen a life of harmony between environmental truth and adventure, you can return here, remove your band and begin wearing the symbol of your people. Remember: the people of SOL will survive in this beautiful land only so long as *most of them find the harmony you seek. It is the dawning of another era, and the future now depends on you.*

Hear my words, my children, and heed them: Brave hearts and calm minds will succeed. Children will never return.

(There is a pause, just long enough to suggest the story is over, then the narrator continues.)

I have one more thing to say to you. Although many joyous adventures await you when you leave this place as a seeker from SOL, your perseverance will be tested many times. If you are to return here and wear the symbol of an adult, then you must begin putting away your childish ways of seeing and doing things. It will not be easy, and there will be times when you feel very much alone.

However, even though you will probably never see me, I will not be far away, for I am of the earth. If you listen closely with your heart you will be able to hear my voice on the wind. And from time to time I will leave some bit of natural beauty in your path to remind you that true beauty comes from the earth, for once you have learned this your life will always be filled with beauty, even if you never return to live among the people of SOL.

Now go.

When the staff member finishes reading, she explains that the Earth Woman's story is a metaphor for the quest the participants are embarking on the next day. They will be seeking ecological understanding and feeling, and striving to craft more harmonious lifestyles, just as these young people did long ago.

Finally, two large clay pieces that fit into the bowl-shaped depressions of the SOL stone, are then presented to the group, revealing a portion of a map. They will complete the map in the morning, after learning how the systems of life are fully integrated on SUNSHIP III. Before they depart in silence, each participant receives a pouch with three natural items to return to their home places, and a small, simulated fishhook on a cord to hang around the neck.

NOTES, CUES AND PROPS

•• Earth Woman's soliloquy is based on the age old story of a journey of exploration and discovery. Its intent is to encourage the SUNSHIP III participants metaphorically to do the same, to venture out beyond their neighborhoods seeking the ideas and insights of people who are trying to live more in harmony with the earth's natural systems and communities.

⊕ ENDANGERED SPECIES ⊕ CEREMONY
(SACRIFICE AND DESTINY)

Awakened just before dawn on the final morning, the participants are told that there is an unusual gathering of creatures taking place in the forest nearby. Led by a candle lantern, they walk sleepily and quietly down a forest trail until they come upon a large clearing. Several silent, dark-clothed ushers motion for them to sit in rows facing a mysterious figure lit only by the light of a single candle lantern on a stump at its feet. The figure stands perfectly still with its back to the newcomers, leaning on a tall wooden staff and dressed in a long, black robe with a large hood covering its head. The hood extends far enough out to hide its face in a black shadow.

When everyone has been seated quietly for a few moments, the figure slowly turns around toward the group, lifting its head as it does, and raps its staff on the ground. It calls out in a low voice...

"THE RENDEZVOUS"

Death: **I am the shadow of death. Who has called me to this place just before the light? Who is dying?**

(From behind a tree off to one side of the audience comes a plaintive reply.)

First Creature: *We beseech you, oh Death. We know that death is natural — that from death comes life — but the humans are killing us all. They are condemning us to eternal death. None will be left to continue our species. Why do they do this?*

Death: **And who are you?**

First Creature: We are the _____. Why do the humans destroy our homes?

Death: (pounding staff) **Ah, arrogance and greed...** (With a deep-throated, slightly eerie edge) **all is arrogance and greed!**

Who else is dying?

(From behind a shrub at the back comes the cautious reply.)

Second Creature: We are dying too, oh Death.

Death: **And who are you?**

Second Creature: We are the blue whales. Why do the humans hunt us relentlessly and destroy our food? They use our bodies to make cosmetics when other substances would do just as well.

Death: (Pounding the staff and cackling slightly.) **Ah, vanity, vanity. All is selfishness and vanity.**

Are there others dying this night?

(From behind a large rock at the other side comes a somewhat challenging cry.)

Third Creature: We cry out to you, oh Death. We are not afraid to die either, but why do the humans want it all? What have we done to them to deserve a death without light? Why must we be banished from the earth forever?

Death: **And who are you?**

Third Creature: We are the peregrine falcons. Why do the humans spray insecticides and chemicals which make our egg shells so thin that they are crushed when we sit on them?

Death: (Pounding the staff again, but in a sad voice.) **Ah, ignorance. Ignorance and greed. All is ignorance and greed.**

(Sonorously) **I am the shadow of death. Who else calls me to this place?**

(From behind a nearby log comes a whispered reply.)

Fourth Creature: We are almost gone...

Death: **Speak, speak!** *(Pounds staff)* **What is it you seek?**

Fourth Creature: We are dying the death of no return as well, and I fear we have come too late. We beseech you, oh Death. It is our last chance.

Death: **Who are you?**

Fourth Creature: We are the sea turtles. We live in the sea and lay our eggs in the sand. The humans eat our eggs and destroy our nesting beaches in their pursuit of pleasure.

Death: (Pounding the staff and almost shrieking this time.) **Ah, avarice. Avarice and carelessness. All is avarice and carelessness.**

(There is a rustling noise behind and to one side of Death.)

All Creatures: (With fear in their voices, not all at the same time, their reactions bounce from one to another, back and forth, over-lapping.) Shhh... What was that? Something comes. (And in a plaintive wail) it is a h·u·m·a·n!

Human: (A third-world voice from farther off in the distance than the creatures' voices, calls out somewhere behind Death, who turns to listen.) Oh, Death. Where are you? Oh, Death, we too are dying. The people in some parts of the world use so much energy and material that there's not enough to go around, and their de-sires encourage us to exploit the other creatures of the earth. What are we to do? Oh, Death, we too suffer... (The human moves across behind Death the whole time it speaks, as if seeking Death. Then the voice fades away as the human moves farther off.) What are we to do...

Death: (Turning back toward the front.) **Go back to your species; I will not take you yet. Tell them to seek out those humans who know — who feel with their hearts. Just as your species sent you to represent them here at the rendezvous point, there are those among the humans who can champion your cause. Speak to them in their hearts — they will hear and respond — but tell them there is not much time. Destiny can be turned aside, but only through sacrifice.**

(An owl hoots.) **Ah, the owl returns home from the hunt. I must go before the light returns...**

NOTES, CUES AND PROPS

•• The "endangered species" should be staff hidden in scattered places behind and to the sides of the audience. Each creature's voice should be different and be unrecognizable to the participants.

•• Choose an endangered specie from your part of the world for the first creature.

•• The tone and pace of Death's voice should vary according to what is being said. Overall, it should be deep and eerie. Pauses at appropriate times are important.

•• At the end Death should turn around and become immobile once again.

•• The event should be timed so that the first light of dawn is breaking on the walk back from the rendezvous.

•• Practice is very important. Timing, volume and quality of the voices, as well as key lines, are crucial to this ceremony's success.

•• Everyone should walk back in silence. Depending on the actual time, participants could have an early Magic Spot time or meet in Sharing Circles before breakfast to process the experience.

•• In processing this activity in Sharing Circles or just in conversation it is important to keep in mind that we are not trying to impose feelings of guilt but rather of care and concern about our impact on the systems of life on our planet. We can lessen our impact; it is not hopeless.

•• We have been working on this experience for fifteen years. It is an original idea, not an adaptation of something else we have seen.

•• If you do this activity at dusk rather than dawn, Death's lines will change slightly. In the first line, it would read: "... who has called me to this place just before the dark...". And the last line would become, "Ah, the owl sets off on its hunt. I must return to the darkness."

•• 1 long black robe with a large hood

•• 1 tall wood staff

•• 1 board for the staff to be pounded on

•• Candle lanterns - 1 next to Death, 1 for the person who leads the group on the trail, a few for the ushers and a few to set out along key spots on the trail.

•• 4 penlights - for the creatures to use, if needed, to read their lines

"TEMPLE OF SOL" — PART TWO
(PREVIEW)

On the final morning, the groups meet their leaders to find out how they will earn the third piece of the SOL stone. They must show that they understand how the integrated systems of life support all living things, and to do that, they must learn to decipher the hieroglyphics.

Divided up into groups of three, each team receives a clay tablet with four lines of glyphs on it, and to their relief, a key to deciphering this pictorial language. Each tablet shows two examples of living things competing for something they need to survive (such as two plants competing for sunlight) and two examples of living things cooperating (like a squirrel that buries acorns, unwittingly planting trees). The teams work together to find real life examples of such interactions in the woods around them, then point them out to a Guide.

Their second task is to build a model that shows they understand how all living things are tied together by the systems of life. Each team gets four strands of yarn (yellow, brown, dark blue, and light blue) and a set of eight glyphs representing parts of the natural processes. Using a branch stuck into the ground for a focal point, they must recreate the flow of sunlight energy and the cycling of air, water and soil (using the bits of coloured yarn and objects they find nearby) to demonstrate how the systems of life work together to support each passenger on the earth. As they tie everything together, they use their glyphs to mark the different parts of the systems (oxygen and carbon dioxide for the air cycle; precipitation, evaporation and transpiration for the water cycle; and decomposition, new growth and nutrients for the soil cycle).

As they work, they recreate the cycles they worked on in the Cycle Factory and the flow of energy from the sun to plants and on to animals which they saw in Solarville. The tree represents all living things, and everything is tied intricately together in the systems of life.

Once they have demonstrated their understanding of the integrated circuits of SUNSHIP III the participants receive the third section of the SOL stone and complete their map. It is a map of the area they are now in, and it leads them a short distance away to another large rock. On this rock they discover another carved glyph, a slightly skewed symbol of harmony like the one they learned about the night before. A quick turn to correct the symbol reveals a secret cylinder cut into the rock, and from it comes a strange map labelled, "The Seekers of Harmony". Places on the map have unusual names like "Safe Haven" and "The Place of the Big Stink", but after some study, it appears to be a map of their own community. But there are many other strange symbols whose meanings will be revealed in the closing ceremony yet to come.

Interrelationships

Living things are grouped together on the earth in specific communities because that is where they can best meet their needs of life. The actual place where something lives in a community, the place where it can meet its needs of life, is called its home or habitat. A habitat may be as small as a beetle's tiny crevice in the bark of a tree or as large as an eagle's vast hunting grounds; a good habitat takes up as much space as the plant or animal needs to find its food, shelter and water.

The role or job in the community performed by a plant or animal is called its niche. A squirrel basically occupies the niche of a tree-climbing seed-eater, while a bat's niche might be described as that of a night-flying insect-eater.

Everything in these communities is somehow connected to everything else. In meeting their needs, all plants and animals are constantly interacting with one another and with their surroundings. It would be impossible for any form of life to exist by itself.

Living things interact with one another in a variety of ways: often they are competing with each other for the same things (as when foxes compete with owls for mice), sometimes they are cooperating, although usually unintentionally (as when a squirrel "accidentally" plants trees as it stores nuts), but invariably they are depending upon one another for some part of their needs.

In reality, everything on earth is tied together in an enormous web of life. Like the web of a spider, when one strand is touched, all the other strands are affected.

⊕ COMMENCEMENT ⊕
(CLOSING)

Everyone has returned to the same room that was used for the opening of the Commencement on the first day. A spotlight comes up on Peter standing at the lectern. The image of the earth as seen from space is projected on the black wall behind him.

"You have now reached the end of these Commencement Exercises. Just as every ending in the natural world is the beginning of another story, so the end of this Commencement marks the beginning of the next stage in your life. The last three days here have been spent preparing you for that passage.

"We have tried to change your perception of our home and the Systems Of Life that support it. When you journeyed to Solarville you learned about the power system of the sunship and the hidden energy costs in everything we do." *(The circular slides used in the opening ceremony appear again as Peter describes what they have been doing.)*

"As workers at the Cycle Factory you saw how the air and water and soil cycles keep the materials that all things are made of moving through the sunship's recycling systems.

"When you helped with the Museum Project you learned about the time system — how everything is constantly changing.

"And at the Temple of SOL you learned about the integrated circuits of the sunship, the ways in which every living and non-living thing is interrelated."

"You have also explored some of the fascinating **S**ections **O**f **L**ife here on board. And we hope you have begun developing richer feelings for the earth and the other life that shares it. You have even heard from some of those other creatures that live on board SUNSHIP III with us.

"Remember your first visit to the Temple of SOL last night? There you heard the story of the People of SOL and their quest for environmental truth, adventure and harmony in their lives. Now it's time for you to set out on a journey of exploration and discovery in your own life."

(The circular slide of the SOL symbol appears again on the black wall, and Peter points out its parts.) "You have learned that this symbol represented environmental truth, adventure and harmony to the People of SOL. The three sections of the symbol are the same as the three sections in the SOL stone. And the entire symbol is surrounded by the rays of the sun, because that is the source of energy for our planet. No one knows for sure, but we believe the three sections also stood for the three great cycles of life — air, water and soil. And that the "Y" that divides them represented the choices one makes — the diverging paths that lie ahead as one moves from being a child into the world of an adult."

Peter returns to the lectern. "Like the young people of SOL, you are about to set out on your own quest searching for how you can live more in harmony with the natural systems and communities of our planet. We call it a Quest because it can be a long and arduous journey and some will fall by the wayside as they seek the path with heart. But, just as with the People of SOL, the future of the earth depends now upon your perseverance.

"Remember the symbol that led you to the secret stone... a circle with a diagonal line through it? *(The image of the SOL symbol is replaced with a circular picture of the harmony symbol.)* That symbol will guide you in the months ahead. It is the symbol of harmony. For truth always comes full circle: it is found in your family, in your school, in your friends. But adventure is daring to leave that circle and test your truths in the world beyond. That is what the young people of SOL had to do, and now, so must you. You must set out alone seeking the harmony that will save the earth.

"Wherever you find this symbol — the circle of truth crossed by the diagonal line of adventure — you will know that you are on the right path. For the symbol of harmony marks the spot where a special natural place or person can be found. You will know such places by their feelings and the people by their actions. Remember though to look with your heart as well as your eyes.

"During your Quest you will be trying to balance your understandings of ecological systems and communities with the rich feelings you can achieve through firsthand experiences with them. The dilemma is that you cannot set off on an adventure in the natural world without having some impact upon it, but you cannot develop deeper feelings for the other life of the earth unless you get out there and have some contact with it. So the truth is in the understandings, the adventure in the feelings and the harmony in the balance you seek between the two.

"The key appears to be to proceed with some caution, while lessening your impact in other areas of your life as you go. So the harmony you seek must also be realized in crafting a new lifestyle for yourself.

"You may have noted in your Ledgers that there are several pages marked with the symbol of harmony. *(Illustrated by a circular slide showing one of the pages in the Ledger for a natural object.)* Three of them are for the natural places where you will return the items in the pouch you received last night at the Temple of SOL. The other three correspond to the characteristics of someone who is living in harmony with the earth *(each illustrated by another circular slide)*: using energy

and materials wisely, demonstrating care for natural places and things, and developing a deeper personal relationship with the earth.

"When you find these people and describe how they are trying to live more in harmony with the earth, they will mark your Ledger with the symbol of SOL before you leave. *(A circular slide appears showing a medallion being pressed onto a page of a Ledger.)* Listen and observe well during your time with them for these people have many ideas you can use in crafting your own lifestyle.

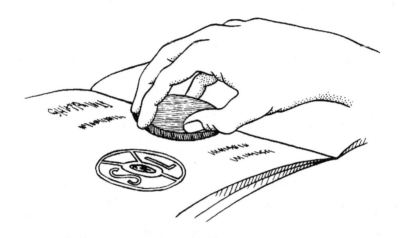

"Remember the fish in the Earth Woman's story? There are two sides to a fish, but you can only see one side at a time. It is really the same with us. There is a harmonious side and a disruptus side to each of us, just like you saw in P/C during the opening of these exercises. The most important choice you each have to make in the coming year is which side you will present to the world. Which side of you will people perceive?

"You will also find in your Ledgers several pages with the scales of a fish where you can note additions to the choices you are making — your own environmental 'thou shalts' and 'thou shalt nots' — which will serve as guideposts for you along the path you have chosen. *(Illustrated by a picture of a page with some of the scales filled in.)* The scales are also there to remind you to use the hook you wear around your neck. However, do not be satisfied with mere appearances; you are no longer a child and you must begin seeking more deeply.

"The pages in one of the last sections of your Ledger are where you must begin describing the lifestyle you are crafting for yourself. *(Circular image of the Ledger pages.)* Your Quest will not end, however, when you have completed those pages; like the Ledger itself they are merely reminders of your journey. Your Quest will end only when you are sure in your heart that you have found the path of harmony and have begun following it in your life. Only then will you be ready to return to the Temple of SOL, remove your wristband and begin wearing the symbol of those who work each day at living more in harmony with the earth. *(Circular slide of SOL symbol.)*

"Everything you have been doing here has been a part of the Commencement Exercises that were designed to prepare you for this great Quest. We have done all we can to help you see the other path and to convince you that it is worth seeking. Now the real choice is up to you. When you get home, you will no longer be required to get permits for all of the energy and materials you use, but that does not mean you aren't using them. Your new perceptions should help you see that you are still a part of those systems every day, in every way. No one will fine you for wasting energy and materials either; from here on, it will be up to you.

"You are the current young people of SOL, in a sense, the crew of our **Ship Of Life**. The time has come for you to choose which direction your life will take, which path you will follow. The fate of our planet is literally in your hands because of the choices you will make in your life. Many environmental scientists now estimate that we only have about 50 years left in which to sort out a more harmonious relationship with the earth. That's your lifetime. So choose wisely.

"Do you remember the map revealed by the SOL stone? It is a map for you to use on your Quest. It will help guide you to the places and people of harmony near you. We have made copies of it for each of those who are ready to begin. We also have wristbands to designate those who will become the new seekers of harmony. If you feel that you are ready to undertake this challenge, please come up and pick up your map and wristband now. Note that together, the band around the rolled up map also forms the harmony symbol — a circle with a line through it — that you will follow on your Quest.

(Each person comes up and gets a rolled up Quest Map bound with a wristband, and shakes hands with the Guides, then sits down. This is done fairly quickly with individuals lining up on one side of the stage and passing across the front. A circular picture of a section of the Quest Map appears on the screen at the rear of the stage, then changes to the earth again as Peter wraps up.)

"I would like for you to meet after this in your Sharing Circles to find out more about your Quest and how you can use the map you received. When your personal Quest is complete, we invite you to return to the Temple of SOL to share the story of your Quest, then remove your wristband, signifying that you have begun acting as a responsible adult and have found the path of harmony. Thus your Commencement ends and your Quest begins."

NOTES, CUES AND PROPS

•• When the Sharing Circles meet, the Guides explain the details of how the Quest works, how the maps are used, what needs to be recorded in the Ledger and so on. And an order form for leftover solarians to obtain items to use on the Quest (bandannas, t-shirts, **The Earth Speaks,** etc.) is given out.

TRAINING - PHASE III
⊕ QUEST ⊕
(SEEKING HARMONY)

At the closing of Commencement the participants each receive a map tied with a wristband to use with the pouch of natural objects and the fishhook they were given at the Temple of SOL. Together, these items set the stage for phase three of their training.

There are three major parts to the Quest: visiting natural places to return objects, interviewing people, and beginning to craft a more harmonious lifestyle.

Throughout the Quest, the Sharing Circles that began meeting at the centre continue to meet on a regular basis. They talk about what they are doing on their Quests and encourage each other in sticking with it.

VISITING NATURAL PLACES

The pouch contains three natural objects, each to be returned to the natural area from which it was taken. Each object, whether a small stone, a seed, a shell, etc., is fairly distinctive and comes from a different area than the other two. The key to the Quest map provides specific directions for everyone, but the participants should be encouraged to go alone. (For example, the key might refer to a park on the map, and note that participants should identify themselves when they arrive so the staff can give them a map of the site showing a more specific location where their item can be returned.) While at each place, the Ledger pages are filled in describing the setting and how the participant feels about it, then the page is stamped with a SOL Seal.

INTERVIEWING ROLE MODELS

Three people are visited, one for each of three categories:

Using energy and materials wisely
Demonstrating care for natural places and things
Developing a deep personal relationship with the earth

The participants ask these people what they are doing in their lives to achieve harmony and then record what they learn in their Ledgers. Afterwards, the person visited stamps their Ledgers with a SOL Seal.

CRAFTING PERSONAL LIFESTYLES

When the three natural objects have been returned and the three people interviewed, the participants decide what to do in the three categories above to begin crafting a more harmonious lifestyle of their own. These choices are recorded in their Ledgers.

RETURNING TO THE TEMPLE OF SOL

When the Quest visits to places and people have been completed, and the personal lifestyle crafting underway for 3-4 months, the Ledger can be sent back to the centre. The staff there examines it to see if the Quest has been successfully undertaken. In some cases they may return the Ledger to the participant with suggestions for additional things to do to make the Quest more meaningful. When the staff feels the participant is ready, an invitation is sent asking the person to return to the Temple of SOL to share the story of the Quest and receive the symbol of SOL. The visit usually takes place about six months (or two seasons) after the first visit. However, receiving the symbol of SOL is not the end of SUNSHIP III. In a way it is the beginning. For now the participants must join others in planning further environmental action — in their schools, at the centre and in the larger community.

The Quest is the most important component of SUNSHIP III. In a sense everything in the programme is designed to prepare and motivate young teens to interact with other people who are trying to live an alternative lifestyle. If the perceptual part of the programme succeeds, the participants will see those they visit as representing choices that can be made in their own lives. Of course, some of those choices may not be acted upon immediately, but all will contribute to an image of what it means to live more lightly on the earth.

The Quest is designed as well to encourage young teens to reach out beyond their peer group and extended family while exploring a different relationship with the earth. Since youngsters at this age are notoriously peer group driven, the Quest should appeal to their sense of adventure and curiosity in prompting them to venture forth on their own. For many of them, this will be the first time they have gone beyond their normal "borders" of family and friends by themselves. We think that's an important part of growing up, leaving the security of the known to experience firsthand another way of living, and SUNSHIP III is specifically positioned to promote it. Every effort should be made to encourage other environmental groups to participate in the journey. This will be a marvelous opportunity for others in the environmental movement to make themselves known to a new generation of trained and motivated teenagers. And earth education depends upon individuals moving beyond crafting their own lifestyle to join in planning actions that will assist everyone in living more harmoniously and joyously with the other life on board this wondrous vessel of life we share.

NOTES, CUES AND PROPS

•• The participants should be able to walk, ride a bike, or take public transportation to most things on the Quest Map. The idea is to get the participants out there exploring on their own rather than relying on someone taking them.

•• The map should be a perceptual tool that is based on the real area where they live but not easily recognizable at first. (It should take some thought to figure out the actual things the names are describing.) "Disguise-removers", like "the place of the big stink" for the sewage treatment plant, will help the participants see things in a different way. (Try describing things the way the People of SOL would have viewed them.) People and places to visit should be indicated on the map in a general fashion.

•• When there are participants from several different areas going through the programme at the same time, they will have to make their own maps based on the sample. They will also need to communicate more with the centre, perhaps having Sharing Circles via the postal system.

•• The SOL Seals for the natural places can be hidden at the sites, held by staff members if they are at centres or parks, or applied by the leader after the participant explains the adventure in a Sharing Circle later.

•• Ideally, the natural objects in the participants' pouches would match up with the natural communities the individual participants had not experienced (as indicated on the checklist in their Ledgers).

•• When setting up the programme a centre should advertise in local environmental newsletters for people who are trying to live in more harmonious ways. The idea is for the participants to be able to meet people who have found a way to eat lower on the food chain, or get around without using much fossil energy, or reuse materials others have thrown away, or are involved in the preservation of a natural area, etc. The participants should ask them what they are doing in their lives to achieve harmony, and then record what they learn in their Ledgers. The person then stamps their Ledger with a SOL Seal. The idea is not necessarily for the participants to copy in their lives what these people are doing, but to get lots of ideas and then to make choices about what they will do in each category (using energy wisely in their recreation, etc.). To prevent those who volunteer to be visited from being besieged by throngs of 13 year olds, the centre should ask each person how many times or how often he or she is willing to be visited and by how many participants at one time. That information can be listed on Quest Cards (providing the appropriate number of sign-in blanks for each volunteer), along with specific instructions on how to find the person and what kinds of questions to ask. The Quest Cards should be placed next to a large Quest Map on the wall of the school or meeting room, and when the participants select who to visit they can sign those they choose as long as there are spaces available. (For those schools whose systems of education may disapprove of teachers encouraging direct contact of this nature, the Guide could arrange for Sharing Circles to meet with the volunteer at a mutually agreed upon site.)

•• In addition to using their maps to find people trying to live more harmonious lifestyles, ask the participants to find several natural areas where they can feel a sense of natural reverence and mark those places on their maps as well. Have them share their impressions of the places they experience, emphasizing why they felt a deep sense of respect and awe when visiting them. Encourage them to take their ledgers with them at these times to record their feelings and then read from them later in a Sharing Circle.

•• Once a year (perhaps on the spring equinox), the centre should host a return by those who have completed their Quest. At the Temple of SOL the participants stand up one at a time to tell a bit about their Quest and the choices they've made. Then they go off to their Magic Spots to bury their wristbands, thus showing that they are ready to live in harmony with the earth as adults.

•• The centre should also arrange special opportunities for those who have completed their Quests, opportunities for them to work together in undertaking local environmental planning and action. These additional training sessions should focus on skills for effecting change as well as guidance and support for specific projects initiated by the participants. This may well be the most demanding phase of the entire programme for it is through this continued contact that you will be able to nurture the most lasting results.

1. "Bluffs of Clay"
2. "Place of the Big Stink"
3. "No Such Thing as Away"
4. "Organic Farm"
5. "Wetland Preserve"
6. "Place of Tall Trees"

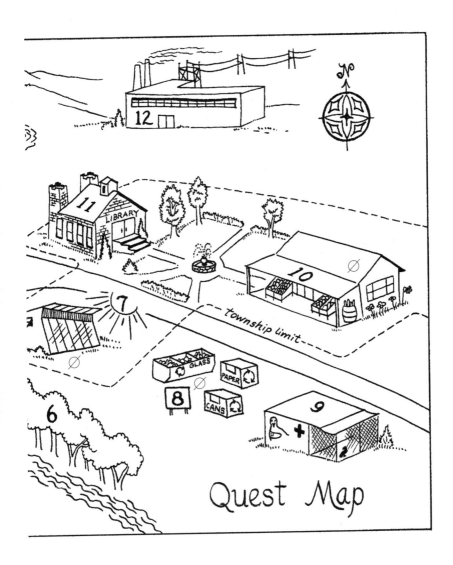

7. "Energy from the Sun"
8. "Reduce, Re-use, Recycle"
9. "Wildlife Hospital"
10. "Harmony Whole Foods Company"
11. "Place of Knowledge"
12. "Fossil Fuel Conversion Site"

A FEW WORDS FOR
TEACHERS AND PARENTS...

Don't worry about the effects of having your students see you in a different role. They will love it, and you will benefit from it when you return. We all have different roles we play in our lives, and it is good for the students to see us in this light. After all, in a sense, we are asking them to play the role of an adult for two days, so it is only natural that we might play a different role as well.

Someone could write a whole volume on leadership tips alone (and perhaps someday we will), but for our purposes here there are three important ways in which you can help us assure success:

- •• treat the participants as adults
- •• help them instead of directing them
- •• enter everything with them enthusiastically

If you can keep these three things uppermost in mind as you carry out your role as a leader, it will make a world of difference in the learners' overall perception of what's happening during these unusual Commencement Exercises. Thanks for all the extra attention you are giving this programme, from all those who made it possible.

LEADERSHIP
LEADER ROLES

Since the entire programme is based on treating the participants as young adults, the "Guides" in SUNSHIP III play a vital role in running this unusual educational experience.

In some cases the teachers and parents involved may have to make a determined effort to change for a couple of days how they have been relating to their students in the past. The motivating power of SUNSHIP III depends upon a significant, occasionally dramatic, shift in how the participants are treated by the adults around them.

Everything possible must be done to move away from a position of taking responsibility for what the participants are doing to a position of being an advisor who is interested in helping out where needed. Please don't direct their actions, but offer to help with their tasks.

Frankly, you must also overlook a bit of bad behaviour (unless it's a clear matter of health and safety) just like you would in a group of adults. In a pinch, you might say something like, "This is your Commencement, but I would suggest...", then let it go at that. Be sure to physically start doing something — anything — at that point to help out though. They must not perceive you as being judgmental, even nonverbally, but primarily a willing supporter of their experience.

There's nothing wrong with making a rather abrupt change in your leadership style, if necessary, to pull off this new role as a "Guide". In fact, it will probably add to its impact, if it is a dramatic shift. Without your assistance in this way, SUNSHIP III will simply not achieve its potential.

For the most part, the programme itself should pull the learners along, but to be completely successful the leaders will have to give themselves over to this "pull" as well. Even if you are not convinced these techniques are the best way to teach, please give them a chance by putting some extra energy into "guiding" your participants through their "exercises".

Please remember that this is a "staged" event, and the participants should know it. We are not trying to convince them that the characters and places introduced in SUNSHIP III are real, but that we have established these elaborate metaphors and analogies to engage them mentally. The success of their "commencement" will depend to a large extent on how much they "perceive" beyond what they see. One of your most important tasks as a leader will be to encourage the participants to talk about all of this among themselves (both during and after the exercises).

⊕ LEADER GUIDELINES ⊕

The following guidelines for programme leaders are the result of many years of observing both leaders and learners in our field. During this time we have learned a great deal ourselves about setting goals, motivating learners, and assuring full participation. Through our observations and study, plus numerous trial and error pilots, a number of insights have evolved. In this brief section we cannot spell out all of these insights in any detail, but we have tried to include the most important aspects. Each of the activity sources cited here includes important information for the leaders who use them, and each activity includes its own "general notes" on conducting the experience. *Earth Education... A New Beginning* also contains an entire chapter on our leader guidelines. However, we can summarize here some "uncommon" things to do when conducting our activities and some "common" things to avoid.

THINGS TO DO

1. Create Magical Learning Adventures

Remember: we want to pull our learners, not push them. To be honest, it's going to take a special effort on your part to create the kind of atmosphere necessary for these activities. We have done a lot of the ground work for you in the way the activities are set up, but much of their success will depend on the special feeling you contribute. Please don't be reluctant to let go a bit, to let the activities pull you along as well as your learners, but then don't add much more "magic" either. We don't want the magic to overwhelm the message. Like a good artist you will have to make sure all the parts work together to produce the intended result. Be sure to establish an atmosphere right from the start that conveys the feeling that these activities are part of an adventure, an adventure that you and your learners are embarking on together.

2. Focus on Sharing and Doing

Remember: it's not what you tell them that's important, but what they do with what you tell them. So it's going to be critical for you to keep the focus on the doing and support the whole effort with the feeling that you are taking on a role in order to share a special experience with your learners. Try to resist that urge to show your participants everything about what is happening. Instead, let the activity itself provide the leadership and pull you and your learners along in discovering and sharing the intended messages together. For teachers leading these activities themselves, this is a tough one. They will have to be both the guide and a member of the team. In this case, work a bit harder at conveying the feeling that you are setting them up for an adventure, and that you really do not know all of the outcomes yourself either.

3. Emphasize the 3 R's: Reward, Reinforce, Relate

Remember: you get the behaviour you reward for. Catch them doing something good and give them a pat on the back. Reinforce the main points by repeating them over and over. That's the fourth R — repetition. Much of a good learning experience takes place after the activity.

Remember: it's what you can do with what you do that counts. When they are not doing the activities, ask them at every opportunity to do something with what they've done. And be sure to help them relate the point of each activity to their own lives. We want them to see how they are a part of these systems, how their actions each day are governed by and impact upon the ecological processes of life. Remember though, our activities are not designed to give the participants a full-blown grasp of the concept. They are designed to build a filing folder that you can fatten up with reinforcing examples later.

4.   Model Positive Environmental Behaviours

Remember: they'll recall what they saw you do long after they have forgotten what you said. Look for ways you can demonstrate good environmental habits yourself. In the end, the students will probably remember some of your personal habits long after they have forgotten whatever you had to say. If you can come across a bit "larger than life" to them, and at the same time demonstrate some sound environmental behaviours that they can easily adopt, then your place in the memory bank of our future leaders is assured. (For ideas, consider what you wear, the tools you carry, what you eat and drink and how it is packaged, simple actions like stopping to smell a flower or making sure the "energy-leaking" lights are off.) Above all, put a sparkle in your eye and a spring in your step! Be careful though that you don't make yourself the message. Lots of programmes in our field confuse their means with their end.

THINGS TO AVOID

1.   Naming and Labelling

Remember: naming is not knowing. Stick to the names of the broad categories of things; most of the others just get in the way. We believe it is more important to focus on the processes of life rather than its pieces. In fact, if you stop and think about it, names are really like landmarks. You just don't need very many of them to find your way. And let's stop repeating those same old mistakes of the past. We think it is a tragedy that most people in our societies can name a few of the trees, birds and such, but can't explain the flow of sunlight energy that supports the life of our planet. While we use some names of things in our activities, for the most part, we either play down their importance or use names that will encourage a different perception of something. Always go for the broadest category possible: a Night-flying insect-eating mammal is far preferable to a Pipistrellus subflavus, and just a Bat is much better than an Eastern Pipistrelle.

2. Talking Without a Focal Point

Remember: most people are visual learners. They need to see something to help them make it more concrete. Talking without a focal point is like learning to swim without water. You could still do it, but why make it so hard on everyone? In these activities, we have tried to make sure there is a focal point whenever the leader is talking. If you find yourself rattling on without something for your learners to look at, chances are good you have begun adlibbing. It is important that you keep the pace of these activities fairly brisk and keep your comments fairly limited.

3. Playing "Twenty-Questions"

Remember: the activity should do the teaching, not the teacher. We believe the task of the teacher is to set up and guide the learners in exciting learning situations. Most of the doing should be done by the students, not the leader. Quizzing the students to work them around to your answer means that you are probably doing most of the doing yourself. Perhaps that's the source of that old adage, "The best way to learn something is to teach it." No wonder, the teachers were doing most of the doing! Frankly, "Twenty-Questions" represents a poor substitute for good doing. Lots of learners don't play, and a few highly verbal, competitive students usually dominate the action. Let's make the task the teacher, and the teacher the guide.

Frankly, this is one of the most difficult of our guidelines to follow. Lots of weak educational activities in this field depend upon the leader to make them do their job afterwards (usually under the guise of "discussion"). We want the point of our learning experiences to be more self-evident for a larger percentage of the participants. And we don't want to risk losing many of the students because the leaders constantly play the "Twenty-Questions" game with them.

Be sure to explain this to your volunteer helpers as well. It's one thing to help the learners relate things to their daily lives, but it's quite another to set up a pressurized atmosphere that destroys the enthusiasm for learning that we are trying so hard to create. Learning "discussions" are definitely our most overworked educational tool and may be our most dangerous. Since kids' imitative abilities are pretty well honed by this age, you can be easily misled in a discussion into thinking that they really are taking away several of ecological understandings from a fairly simple activity. It is most likely untrue. Besides, a primary reason why we forget an estimated 90% of what we learn in school is probably because such a large amount of what we supposedly absorbed took place in discussions that were not well-grounded in relevant, concrete actions. If we are going to go to all of the trouble to take classes outside to begin with, let's not spend our time out there in lengthy discussions with just a few students.

4. Drifting Into Activity Entropy

Remember: pay attention to the details. All the props and roles and techniques serve as tools to help you do your job. A craftsman with no tools is going to have a tough time building anything. Don't carelessly throw away the smallest item until you are sure you have a thorough grasp of your job and your product.

Remember: the first rule of tinkering is to save all the parts. It's easy to decide to eliminate some of the props or change some of the roles in our activities, rationalizing that they are not really crucial to the experience, or to make do with an inadequate prop when a little more effort would produce a really good one. Of course, no one can say at exactly what point an activity will be so diminished by one of the changes that it will cease to do its job. Energetic leaders can get away with a lot, even if it means they burn out sooner themselves.

We believe that the props and roles utilized in our activities are integral parts, chosen for their ability to intensify and sharpen the learning experiences. Please be sensitive to all the little details, and let the programme work for you. We think you'll be pleasantly surprised at the results.

SUPPORT

The difference between a great earth education programme and a merely satisfactory one is often in the attention being paid to the details. So once you have the basic structure of your programme underway, you will need to start polishing its supportive elements. Or as someone else so aptly put it, the difference between the ordinary and the extraordinary is in that little extra. In great earth education programmes that little extra can often be found in what's being done during the daily routines.

If earth education programmes exist to change people's relationship with the earth, then the sites where they are offered, and the staff that conduct them, must provide witness that they are working on improving their own relationship as well. Of course, this will mean different things in different places. What is important is not that we have all achieved some utopian state before we can offer an earth education programme, but that we are conscious of our own struggle to grow more in harmony with the earth's natural systems and communities. Above all else, our participants need to know that we are facing our own shortcomings as honestly as we are asking them to face theirs. With that in mind, here are some ideas for where we can begin.

⊕ TIME OUT ⊕
(PULLING BACK)

Our learning programmes are intense. That's the idea. They are supposed to be powerful springboard experiences that catapult motivated learners back to their classrooms (and bedrooms) to continue making changes in their lives. Earth education programmes are not primarily recreational nor social outings.

Not surprisingly then, your participants will need some down time. Maybe it will be just a chance to slow up for a while, to take a walk or a photograph, or maybe it will require something a bit more strenuous, like exploring "the unknown territory" or engaging in a non- or low-competitive game. Whatever the options they should provide a break where the participants can choose what to do with their time (some may just want to visit their Magic Spots again).

This is a good opportunity for getting the teachers or other adult leaders involved as well. They can organize some of the choices and explain them after lunch each day. In that case, however, please ask them to avoid heavy duty learning inputs during this period. We don't want to load up the learners with more to ponder. (Low-key experiential sessions are okay as long as they complement the programme.) You will need to monitor this very carefully.

⊕ MEALS ⊕
(DEMONSTRATING BEHAVIOURS)

Mealtimes are great times for demonstrating ways of living more lightly on the earth. Once again, it's not enough for us to just talk about lessening our impact, our learners need to see concrete examples of how we're trying to accomplish this ourselves. At every meal there should be a brief input on the choices the site has made and why. The hidden costs like those revealed in Mario's Pizza Parlour, should be examined at every table each day. Our participants need to see that there are always choices to be made, but they're not always easy ones. Have the cook describe some of the problems. Ask the participants to make recommendations. Monitor the site's waste.

Suggest that food is a gift that's actually produced by the natural systems and communities of the earth, not by its human passengers, and thus we should give thanks each morning to our kin for nourishing us. As a sentient top predator we can work with the earth's natural systems, and within the natural communities where they operate, to draw forth our own food supplies on board this sunship we share, or we can unthinkingly exploit our fellow passengers for our short-term gain. Food is not something we produce; it is something we take.

In an earth education programme eating lower on the food chain must be our first dietary guideline. Avoiding saturated fats and refined sugars could be our second. Demonstrating choices that our participants can make in their daily lives should be our third. We can't change every kitchen overnight, but we can start. And we can discuss openly the problems we are having in doing so. Better yet, we can invite the participants to play a role. They can prepare guidelines for any snack food future learners bring with them when they come. They can "test" new menu items and tell the cooks what they conclude. They can cut back on their own consumption.

⊕ EVENING WORKSHOPS ⊕
(EXAMINING ALTERNATIVES)

Evening workshops offer another opportunity for involving teachers or other adult leaders, plus volunteers from the community, in planning and carrying out a vital element of SUNSHIP III.

Workshops should focus on specific things young people can do in their own daily routines to live more lightly on the earth. Take your lead from the "Billy's Day" skit. It presents lots of possibilities, from evaluating personal toiletries to the optimal length of a shower.

Wherever possible set up these sessions as skill-building opportunities. Give the participants something they can practice doing, instead of just discussing. Maybe it's actually preparing an alternative sack lunch for the next day or making their own snack food. How about a session on reading clothing labels (asking them to provide the samples from things they brought with them)? Or consider a session on using sample restaurant menus to practice ordering a "living more lightly" meal.

The important thing is to use the actual items young people come into contact with almost every day. Examine alternatives for paper, pencils and pens, notebooks. Analyze the hidden energy costs of various recreational sports. Set up a couple of sample clothing racks and ask teams to choose an outfit for eco-harmonious (again, using clothing choices provided by the leaders and participants). Put together an exhibit of things with plugs (incorporating as many samples as possible from those the participants brought with them) and ask them what they would be willing to give up and why.

LIGHTS OUT

Many outdoor centres tend to relinquish any responsibilities for one of the most crucial parts of the day: bedtime. They turn this over to the teachers and the adults accompanying them with no programmatic suggestions whatsoever. As a result lots of participants roll out for the next day's activities having had very little sleep.

Since we are treating our participants as adults in SUNSHIP III, we cannot establish an arbitrary bedtime for them, but we can incorporate a programme element into the closing of each day. For example, ask everyone to be in bed by a certain time because you want to share some thoughts with them from **The Earth Speaks** so they will have something to ponder in their dreams. Make this an integral part of the programme, not the routines.

THE JOURNEY AHEAD

SUNSHIP III is based on a simple premise: Teenagers are entering a crucial phase of their lives, and we should recognize that step of their journey. As young adults they are making important choices that will have a lasting effect on the earth. As experienced adults we can celebrate their new status with them, but also challenge them to look beyond the surface to perceive how things are being presented to them.

We want the participants in SUNSHIP III to respond to our efforts at both the imaginative and intellectual levels. If we are successful, they will contemplate both the whats and the ways of our programme. And they will begin realizing that they have significant choices to make about their personal impact upon the planet we share in this corner of the universe.

There is no special formula for achieving the harmonious yet joyous lifestyle that a biotically rich planet can sustain. There is only intent and skepticism and ecological feeling, filtered by our perception. Our intent is to remove some disguises for our learners about the real costs of their lifestyles. Our skepticism is to offset the commercial and management messages young people are innundated with every day, even in their own classrooms. Our ecological feeling is to do more to help teenagers develop a less consumptive and more tactile relationship with the natural world. Our perceptual filter is seeing the earth as a wondrous Song Of Life filled with marvelous melodies. We could use your voice.

IMPLEMENTING THE SUNSHIP III PROGRAMME

The Institute for Earth Education offers a required programme package for those interested in sponsoring SUNSHIP III. A programme package contains the masters (along with permission to print the copyrighted materials) for such things as the Guidebook and Ledger as well as the slide show and chorus tape for the commencement ceremonies. Sets of materials that each participant receives, like the fishhook and wristband, are also provided by I•E•E for those who have purchased the programme package.

For an information packet on obtaining a programme package to set up SUNSHIP III, contact the Major Branch office of I•E•E nearest you.

The Institute for Earth Education
Cedar Cove, Greenville, WV 24945 U.S.A.

INDEX

H

I

L

M

O

P

Q

R

S

T

U

W